Level Four
D / Grade 2½

HYMNS and GOSPEL SONGS

for Piano or Organ

compiled, arranged and edited by
John W. Schaum

• Sing-Along, Play-Along •

INDEX

Abide With Me 22
All Hail the Power of Jesus' Name 3
Amazing Grace 13
Blessed Assurance 17
Blest Be the Tie That Binds 21
Chord-Along Dictionary 2
Face to Face 11
Fairest Lord Jesus 9
Faith of Our Fathers 19
He Leadeth Me 18
Holy, Holy, Holy 8
I Love to Tell the Story 14
Jesus, Lover of My Soul 16
Mighty Fortress Is Our God, A 6
Nearer, My God, to Thee 10
Onward, Christian Soldiers 7
O That Will Be Glory 15
Rock of Ages 5
Sing-Along Lyric Sheets 23
Softly and Tenderly 12
Sweet Hour of Prayer 20
What a Friend We Have In Jesus 4

EXCLUSIVELY DISTRIBUTED BY
HAL•LEONARD®
CORPORATION
7777 W. BLUEMOUND RD. P.O. BOX 13819 MILWAUKEE, WI 53213

© Copyright 1960, Renewed 1988 by Schaum Publications, Inc., Mequon, Wisconsin
International Copyright Secured • All Rights Reserved • Printed in U.S.A.

Schaum Chord Dictionary

C

C	Cm	C+
CEG	CE♭G	CEG♯

C6	Cm6	C7
CEGA	CE♭GA	CEGB♭

Cdim7	Cmaj7	Cm7
CE♭G♭A	CEGB	CE♭GB♭

Cm7-5	C+7	C9
CE♭G♭B♭	CEG♯B♭	CEGB♭D

D♭

D♭	D♭m	D♭+
D♭F A♭	D♭F♭A♭	D♭F A

D♭6	D♭m6	D♭7
D♭F A♭B♭	D♭F♭A♭B♭	D♭F A♭C♭

D♭dim7	D♭maj7	D♭m7
D♭E G B♭	D♭F A♭C	D♭F♭A♭C♭

D♭m7-5	D♭+7	D♭9
D♭F♭A♭♭C♭	D♭F A C♭	D♭F A♭C♭E♭

D

D	Dm	D+
DF♯A	DFA	DF♯A♯

D6	Dm6	D7
DF♯AB	DFAB	DF♯AC

Ddim7	Dmaj7	Dm7
DFG♯B	DF♯AC♯	DFAC

Dm7-5	D+7	D9
DFA♭C	DF♯A♯C	DF♯ACE

E♭

E♭	E♭m	E♭+
E♭G B♭	E♭G♭B♭	E♭G B

E♭6	E♭m6	E♭7
E♭G B♭C	E♭G♭B♭C	E♭G B♭D♭

E♭dim7	E♭maj7	E♭m7
E♭G♭A C	E♭G B♭D	E♭G♭B♭D♭

E♭m7-5	E♭+7	E♭9
E♭G♭B♭♭D♭	E♭G B D♭	E♭G B♭D♭F

E

E	Em	E+
EG♯B	EGB	EG♯B♯

E6	Em6	E7
EG♯BC♯	EGBC♯	EG♯BD

Edim7	Emaj7	Em7
EG B♭D♭	EG♯BD♯	EGBD

Em7-5	E+7	E9
EGB♭D	EG♯B♯D	EG♯BDF♯

F

F	Fm	F+
FAC	FA♭C	FAC♯

F6	Fm6	F7
FACD	FA♭CD	FACE♭

Fdim7	Fmaj7	Fm7
FA♭BD	FACE	FA♭CE♭

Fm7-5	F+7	F9
FA♭C♭E♭	FAC♯E♭	FACE♭G

G♭

G♭	G♭m	G♭+
G♭B♭D♭	G♭B♭♭D♭	D♭G♭B♭D

G♭6	G♭m6	G♭7
G♭B♭D♭E♭	G♭B♭♭D♭E♭	G♭B♭D♭F♭

G♭dim7	G♭maj7	G♭m7
G♭ACE♭	G♭B♭D♭F	G♭B♭♭D♭F♭

G♭m7-5	G♭+7	G♭9
G♭B♭♭D♭♭F♭	G♭B♭DF♭	G♭B♭♭D♭F♭A♭

G

G	Gm	G+
GBD	GB♭D	GBD♯

G6	Gm6	G7
GBDE	GB♭DE	GBDF

Gdim7	Gmaj7	Gm7
GB♭D♭E	GBDF♯	GB♭DF

Gm7-5	G+7	G9
GB♭D♭F	GBD♯F	GBDFA

A♭

A♭	A♭m	A♭+
A♭C E♭	A♭C♭E♭	A♭C E

A♭6	A♭m6	A♭7
A♭C E♭F	A♭C♭E♭F	A♭C E♭G♭

A♭dim7	A♭maj7	A♭m7
A♭BDF	A♭C E♭G	A♭C♭E♭G♭

A♭m7-5	A♭+7	A♭9
A♭C E♭♭G♭	A♭C E G♭	A♭C E♭G♭B♭

A

A	Am	A+
AC♯E	ACE	AC♯E♯

A6	Am6	A7
AC♯EF♯	ACEF♯	AC♯EG

Adim7	Amaj7	Am7
ACE♭G♭	AC♯EG♯	ACEG

Am7-5	A+7	A9
ACE♭G	AC♯E♯G	AC♯EGB

B♭

B♭	B♭m	B♭+
B♭DF	B♭D♭F	B♭DF♯

B♭6	B♭m6	B♭7
B♭DFG	B♭D♭FG	B♭DFA♭

B♭dim7	B♭maj7	B♭m7
B♭D♭EG	B♭DFA	B♭D♭FA♭

B♭m7-5	B♭+7	B♭9
B♭D♭F♭A♭	B♭DF♯A♭	B♭DFA♭C

B

B	Bm	B+
BD♯F♯	BDF♯	BD♯Fx

B6	Bm6	B7
BD♯F♯G♯	BDF♯G♯	BD♯F♯A

Bdim7	Bmaj7	Bm7
BDFA♭	BD♯F♯A♯	BDF♯A

Bm7-5	B+7	B9
BDFA	BD♯Fx A	BD♯F♯AC♯

For F♯ chords use G♭   For G♯ chords use A♭
For C♯ chords use D♭   For D♯ chords use E♭

The letter names of the chords may be rearranged (inverted) if necessary. Example:

For ease of note-reading, some of the chords above (especially diminished 7ths) have been notated enharmonically.

1. All Hail the Power of Jesus' Name

EDWARD PERRONET
Maestoso

OLIVER HOLDEN
arr. by John W. Schaum

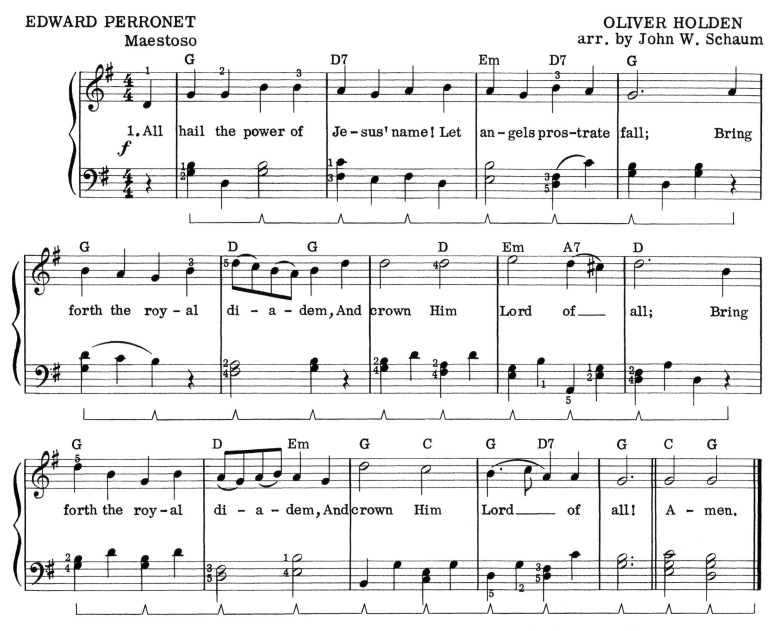

2. Ye chosen seed of Israel's race,
Ye ransomed from the fall,
Hail Him who saves you by His grace,
And crown Him Lord of all;
Hail Him who saves you by His grace
And crown Him Lord of all!

3. Let every kindred, every tribe,
On this terrestrial ball,
To Him all majesty ascribe,
And crown Him Lord of all;
To Him all majesty ascribe,
And crown Him Lord of all!

4. O that with yonder sacred throng
We at His feet may fall!
We'll join the everlasting song,
And crown Him Lord of all;
We'll join the everlasting song,
And crown Him Lord of all!

SUGGESTIONS for USE of CHORDS - at PIANO and ORGAN

For PIANO:	*Right Hand:*	Play treble clef melody as written, or in octaves.
	Left Hand:	Improvise an accompaniment (based on chord symbols). Consult "Chord Dictionary" on page 2.
For ORGAN:	*Upper Manual.*	Right hand plays melody as written.
	Lower Manual:	Left hand improvises and accompaniment (based on chord symbols).
	Pedal:	Play root of each chord (or - alternate tonic and dominant of each chord).
For CHORD ORGAN or PIANO ACCORDION:		Make the same adjustments as indicated for piano.
For GUITAR:		Improvise an animated strum accompaniment based on the chord symbols.

2. What a Friend We Have in Jesus

JOSEPH SCRIVEN
Moderato

CHARLES C. CONVERSE
arr. by John W. Schaum

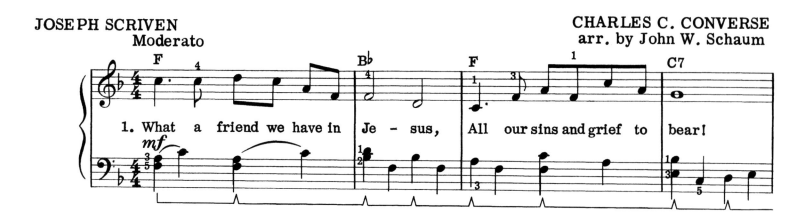

2. Have we trials and temptations?
   Is there trouble anywhere?
   We should never be discouraged,
   Take it to the Lord in pray'r.
   Can we find a friend so faithful
   Who will all our sorrows share?
   Jesus knows our ev'ry weakness,
   Take it to the Lord in pray'r.

3. Are we weak and heavy laden,
   Cumbered with a load of care?
   Precious Saviour, still our refuge,
   Take it to the Lord in pray'r.
   Do thy friends despise, forsake thee?
   Take it to the Lord in pray'r;
   In His arms He'll take and shield thee
   Thou will find a solace there.

3. Rock of Ages

AUGUSTUS M. TOPLADY
Andante

THOMAS HASTINGS
arr. by John W. Schaum

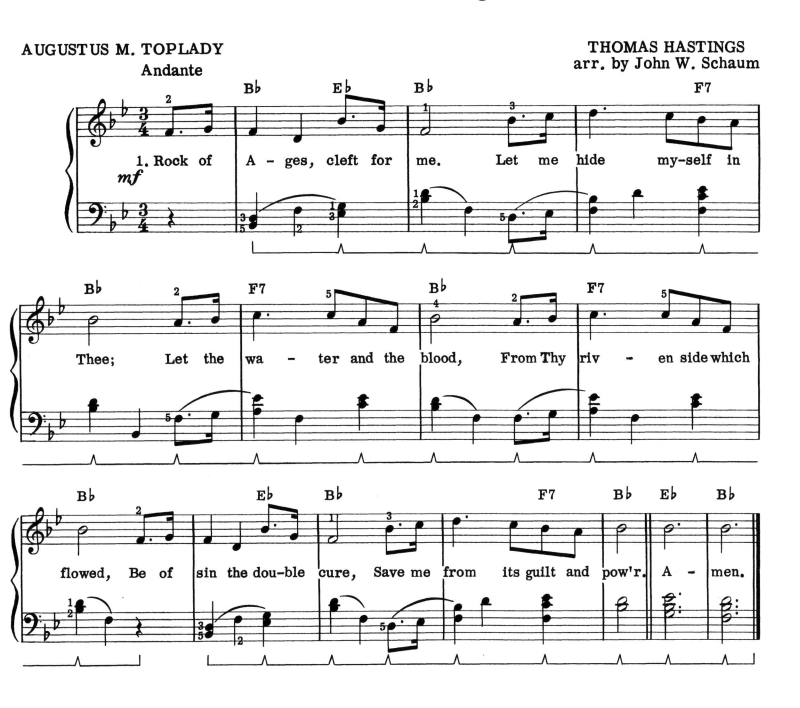

2. Not the labor of my hands
   Can fulfill Thy law's demands;
   Could my zeal no respite know,
   Could my tears forever flow,
   All for sin could not atone;
   Thou must save, and Thou alone.

3. Nothing in my hand I bring,
   Simply to Thy cross I cling;
   Naked, come to Thee for dress;
   Helpless, look to Thee for grace;
   Foul, I to the fountain fly,
   Wash me, Savior, or I die.

4. While I draw this fleeting breath,
   When mine eyes shall close in death,
   When I soar to worlds unknown,
   See Thee on Thy judgment throne,
   Rock of Ages, cleft for me,
   Let me hide myself in Thee.

4. A Mighty Fortress Is Our God

MARTIN LUTHER
arr. by John W. Schaum

Andante

f 1. A might-y for-tress is—our God, A bul-wark nev-er fail - ing; Our

help - er He,—a - mid— the flood Of mor-tal ills pre - vail - ing. For

still our an - cient foe Doth seek to work us woe; His craft and power are

great, And, armed with cru - el hate, On earth is not his e - qual. A - men.

2. Did we in our own strength confide,
   Our striving would be losing,
   Were not the right Man on our side,
   The Man of God's own choosing.
   Dost ask who that may be?
   Christ Jesus, it is He;
   Lord Sabaoth is His name,
   From age to age the same,
   And He must win the battle.

3. And though this world, with devils filled,
   Should threaten to undo us,
   We will not fear, for God hath willed
   His truth to triumph through us.
   The prince of darkness grim –
   We tremble not for him;
   His rage we can endure,
   For lo! his doom is sure:
   One little word shall fell him.

4. That word above all earthly powers –
   No thanks to them – abideth;
   The Spirit and the gifts are ours
   Thro' Him who with us sideth.
   Let goods and kindred go,
   This mortal life also;
   The body they may kill;
   God's truth abideth still,
   His kingdom is forever.

5. Onward, Christian Soldiers

SABINE BARING-GOULD

ARTHUR SULLIVAN
arr. by John W. Schaum

2. Like a mighty army
   Moves the Church of God;
   Brothers, we are treading
   Where the saints have trod;
   We are not divided;
   All one body we,
   One in hope and doctrine,
   One in charity. Refrain

3. Crowns and thrones may perish,
   Kingdoms rise and wane,
   But the Church of Jesus
   Constant will remain.
   Gates of hell can never
   'Gainst that Church prevail;
   We have Christ's own promise,
   And that cannot fail. Refrain

4. Onward, then, ye people,
   Join our happy throng,
   Blend with ours your voices
   In the triumph song;
   Glory, laud, and honor,
   Unto Christ the King:
   This thro' countless ages
   Men and angels sing. Refrain

6. Holy, Holy, Holy

REGINALD HEBER

Rev. JOHN B. DYKES
arr. by John W. Schaum

2. Holy, Holy, Holy! All the saints adore Thee,
   Casting down their golden crowns around the glassy sea;
   Cherubim and seraphim falling down before Thee,
   Who wert, and art, and evermore shalt be.

3. Holy, Holy, Holy. Tho' the darkness hide Thee,
   Tho' the eye of sinful man Thy glory may not see,
   Only Thou art holy; there is none beside Thee
   Perfect in pow'r, in love, in purity.

4. Holy, Holy, Holy, Lord God Almighty!
   All Thy works shall praise Thy name in earth, and sky, and sea;
   Holy, Holy, Holy! Merciful and Mighty!
   God in Three Persons, blessed Trinity!

7. Fairest Lord Jesus

RICHARD S. WILLIS
arr. by John W. Schaum

1. Fair - est Lord Je - sus, Rul - er of all na - ture,

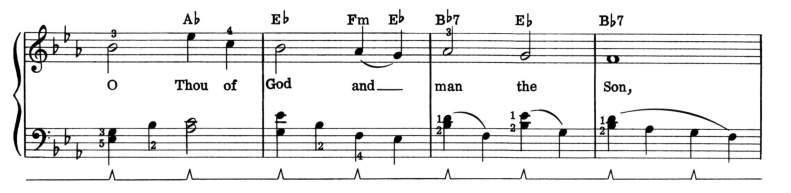

O Thou of God and man the Son,

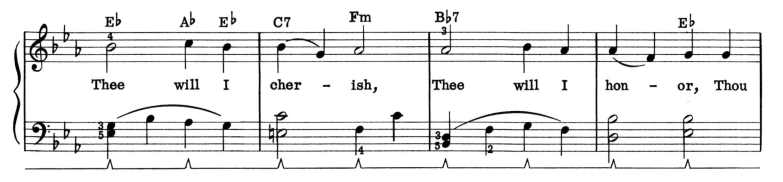

Thee will I cher - ish, Thee will I hon - or, Thou

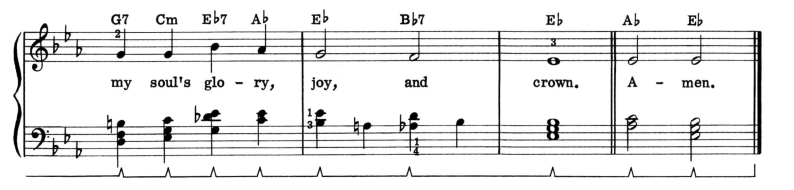

my soul's glo - ry, joy, and crown. A - men.

2. Fair are the meadows,
   Fairer still the woodlands,
   Robed in the blooming garb of spring;
   Jesus is fairer,
   Jesus is purer,
   Who makes the woeful heart to sing.

3. Fair is the sunshine,
   Fairer still the moonlight,
   And all the twinkling, starry host;
   Jesus shines brighter,
   Jesus shines purer,
   Than all the angels heaven can boast.

8. Nearer, My God to Thee

SARAH F. ADAMS
Andantino

LOWELL MASON
arr. by John W. Schaum

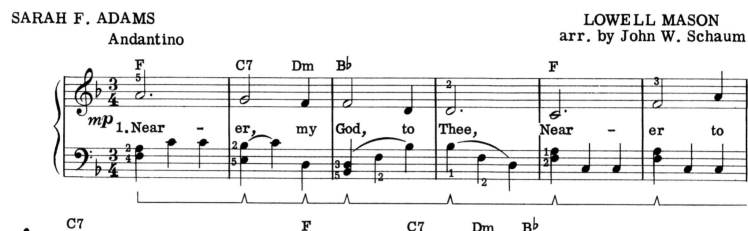

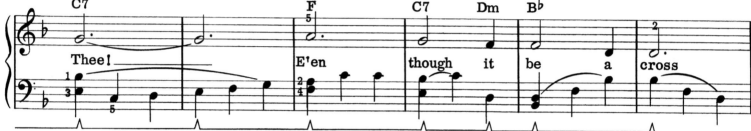

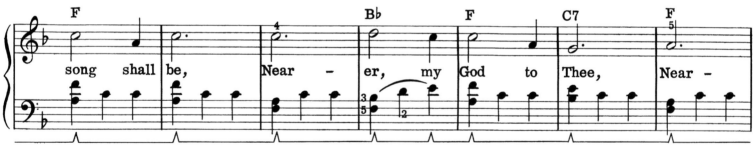

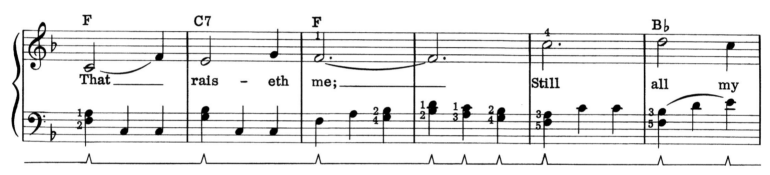

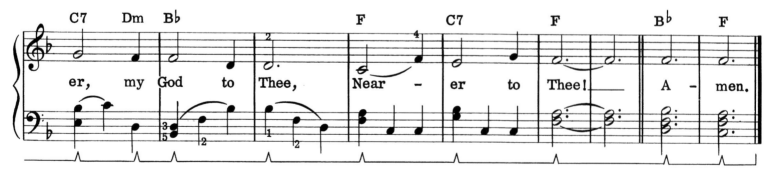

2. Though like the wanderer,
The sun gone down,
Darkness be over me,
My rest a stone;
Yet in all my dreams I'd be
Nearer, my God, to Thee,
Nearer, my God, to Thee,
Nearer to Thee!

3. There let the way appear,
Steps unto heaven:
All that Thou sendest me,
In mercy given:
Angels to beckon me
Nearer, my God, to Thee,
Nearer, my God, to Thee,
Nearer to Thee!

4. Then with my waking thoughts
Bright with Thy praise,
Out of my stony griefs
Bethel I'll raise;
So by my woes to be
Nearer, my God, to Thee,
Nearer, my God, to Thee,
Nearer to Thee!

5. Or if on joyful wing,
Cleaving the sky,
Sun, moon, and stars forgot,
Upward I fly,
Still all my song shall be,
Nearer, my God, to Thee,
Nearer, my God, to Thee,
Nearer to Thee!

9. Face to Face

Mrs. FRANK A. BRECK

GRANT COLFAX TULLAR
arr. by John W. Schaum

1. Face to face with Christ my Sav - iour, Face to face what will it be. When with rap-ture I be - hold Him, Je - sus Christ who died for me?

Refrain

Face to face I shall be - hold Him, Far be-yond the star-ry sky; Face to face in all His glo - ry, I shall see Him by and by. A - men.

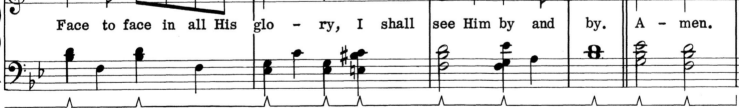

2. Only faintly now I see Him,
   With the darkling veil between;
   But a blessed day is coming,
   When His glory shall be seen. Refrain

3. What rejoicing in His presence,
   When are banished grief and pain;
   When the crooked ways are straightened,
   And the dark things shall be plain. Refrain

4. Face to face! O blissful moment!
   Face to face - to see and know;
   Face to face with my Redeemer,
   Jesus Christ who loves me so. Refrain

10. Softly and Tenderly

WILL. L. THOMPSON
arr. by John W. Schaum

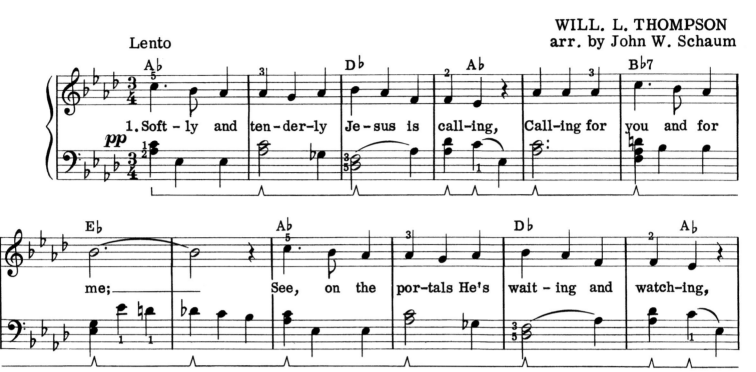

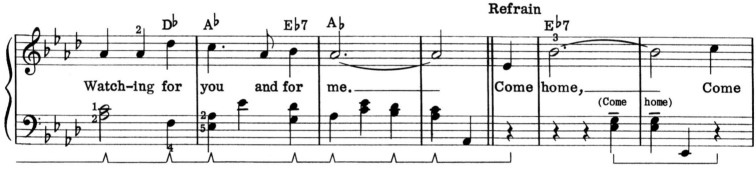

2. Why should we tarry when Jesus is pleading,
   Pleading for you and for me?
   Why should we linger and heed not His mercies,
   Mercies for you and for me? Refrain

3. Time is now fleeting, the moments are passing,
   Passing from you and from me;
   Shadows are gathering, death-beds are coming,
   Coming for you and for me. Refrain

4. Oh! for the wonderful love He has promised,
   Promised for you and for me;
   Tho' we have sinned, He has mercy and pardon,
   Pardon for you and for me. Refrain

11. Amazing Grace

JOHN NEWTON
arr. by John W. Schaum

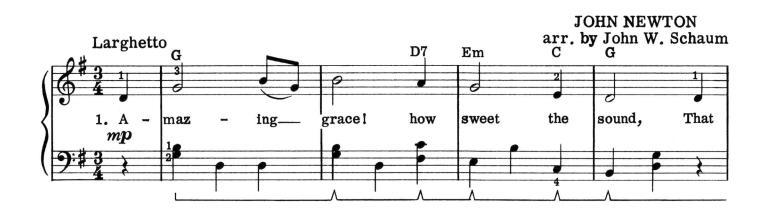

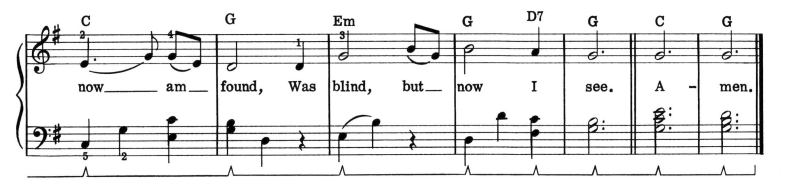

2. 'Twas grace that taught my heart to fear,
   And grace my fears relieved;
   How precious did that grace appear
   The hour I first believed!

3. Thru many dangers, toils and snares,
   I have already come;
   'Tis grace hath bro't me safe thus far,
   And grace will lead me home.

4. When we've been there ten thousand years,
   Bright shining as the sun,
   We've no less days to sing God's praise
   Than when we first begun.

12. I Love to Tell the Story

KATHERINE HANKEY

WILLIAM G. FISCHER
arr. by John W. Schaum

2. I love to tell the story,
   More wonderful it seems
   Than all the golden fancies
   Of all our golden dreams.
   I love to tell the story,
   It did so much for me;
   And that is just the reason
   I tell it now to thee. Refrain

3. I love to tell the story,
   'Tis pleasant to repeat
   What seems, each time I tell it,
   More wonderfully sweet.
   I love to tell the story,
   For some have never heard
   The message of salvation
   From God's own holy Word. Refrain

4. I love to tell the story,
   For those who know it best
   Seem hungering and thirsting
   To hear it like the rest.
   And when, in scenes of glory,
   I sing the new, new song,
   'Twill be the old, old story
   That I have loved so long. Refrain

13. O That Will Be Glory

CHARLES H. GABRIEL
arr. by John W. Schaum

1. When all my la-bors and tri-als are o'er, And I am safe on that beau-ti-ful shore, Just to be near the dear Lord I a-dore, Will thro' the a-ges be glo-ry for me.

Refrain: O that will be glo-ry for me, glo-ry for me, Glo-ry for me, glo-ry for me, glo-ry for me, glo-ry for me; When by His grace I shall look on His face, That will be glo-ry, be glo-ry for me. A-men.

2. When, by the gift of His infinite grace,
   I am accorded in heaven a place,
   Just to be there and to look on His face,
   Will thro' the ages be glory for me. <u>Refrain</u>

3. Friends will be there I have loved long ago;
   Joy like a river around me will flow;
   Yet, just a smile from my Savior, I know,
   Will thro' the ages be glory for me. <u>Refrain</u>

14. Jesus Lover of My Soul

CHARLES WESLEY

SIMEON B. MARSH
arr. by John W. Schaum

Moderato

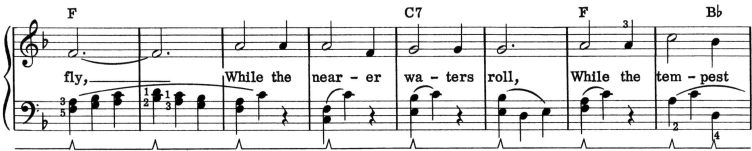

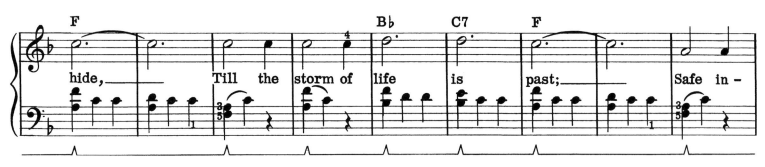

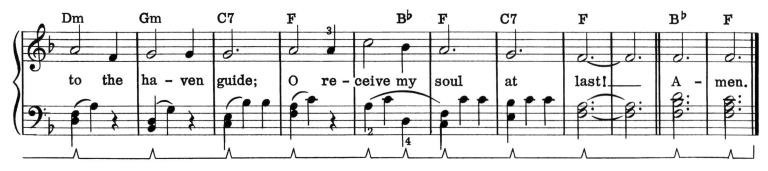

2. Other refuge have I none;
Hangs my helpless soul on Thee;
Leave, ah! leave me not alone,
Still support and comfort me.
All my trust on Thee is stayed,
All my help from Thee I bring;
Cover my defenseless head
With the shadow of Thy wing.

3. Thou, O Christ, art all I want;
More than all in Thee I find:
Raise the fallen, cheer the faint,
Heal the sick, and lead the blind.
Just and holy is Thy name;
I am all unrighteousness;
False and full of sin I am,
Thou art full of truth and grace.

4. Plenteous grace with Thee is found,
Grace to cover all my sin;
Let the healing streams abound;
Make and keep me pure within.
Thou of life the Fountain art,
Freely let me take of Thee;
Spring Thou up within my heart.
Rise to all eternity.

15. Blessed Assurance

FANNY CROSBY

Mrs. JOS. F. KNAPP
arr. by John W. Schaum

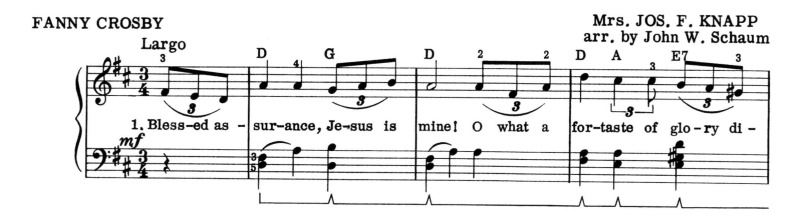

1. Bless-ed as - sur-ance, Je-sus is mine! O what a for-taste of glo-ry di-

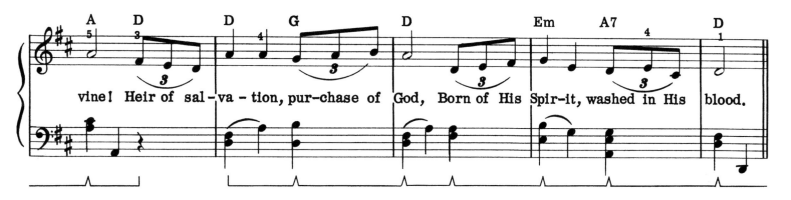

vine! Heir of sal-va-tion, pur-chase of God, Born of His Spir-it, washed in His blood.

Refrain

This is my sto-ry, this is my song, Prais-ing my Sav-iour all the day long; This is my

sto-ry, this is my song, Prais-ing my Sav-iour all the day long. A - men.

2. Perfect submission, perfect delight,
   Visions of rapture now burst on my sight!
   Angels descending, bring from above
   Echoes of mercy, whispers of love. <u>Refrain</u>

3. Perfect submission, all is at rest,
   I in my Saviour am happy and blest;
   Watching and waiting, looking above,
   Filled with His goodness, lost in His love. <u>Refrain</u>

16. He Leadeth Me

JOSEPH H. GILMORE
Andante

WILLIAM B. BRADBURY
arr. by John W. Schaum

2. Sometimes 'mid scenes of deepest gloom,
   Sometimes where Eden's bowers bloom,
   By waters still, o'er troubled sea,
   Still 'tis His hand that leadeth me! Refrain

3. Lord, I would clasp Thy hand in mine,
   Nor ever murmur nor repine,
   Content, whatever lot I see,
   Since 'tis my God that leadeth me! Refrain

4. And when my task on earth is done,
   When, by Thy grace, the victory's won,
   E'en death's cold wave I will not flee,
   Since God thro' Jordan leadeth me. Refrain

17. Faith of Our Fathers

FREDERICK W. FABER

Maestoso

HENRY F. HEMY
arr. by John W. Schaum

1. Faith of our fa - thers! liv - ing still In spite of dun - geon,

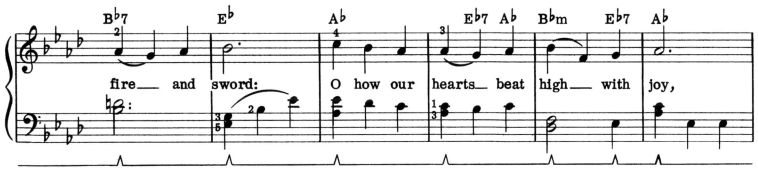

fire___ and sword: O how our hearts___ beat high___ with joy,

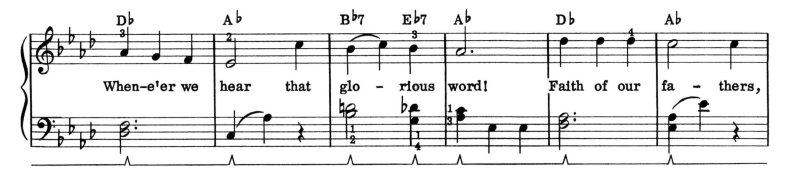

When-e'er we hear that glo - rious word! Faith of our fa - thers,

ho - ly faith! We will be true to thee till death. A - men.

2. Our fathers, chained in prisons dark,
   Were still in heart and conscience free:
   How sweet would be their children's fate,
   If they, like them, could die for thee!
   Faith of our fathers, holy faith!
   We will be true to thee till death!

3. Faith of our fathers! God's great power
   Shall win all nations unto thee,
   And through the truth that comes from God
   Mankind shall then indeed be free:
   Faith of our fathers, holy faith!
   We will be true to thee till death!

4. Faith of our fathers! we will love
   Both friend and foe in all our strife:
   And preach thee, too, as love knows how,
   By kindly words and virtuous life:
   Faith of our fathers, holy faith!
   We will be true to thee till death!

18. Sweet Hour of Prayer

W. W. WALFORD

WILLIAM B. BRADBURY
arr. by John W. Schaum

Moderato

2. Sweet hour of prayer! sweet hour of prayer!
Thy wings shall my petition bear
To Him whose truth and faithfulness
Engage the waiting soul to bless;
And since He bids me seek His face,
Believe His Word and trust His grace,
I'll cast on Him my every care,
And wait for thee, sweet hour of prayer.

3. Sweet hour of prayer! sweet hour of prayer!
May I thy consolation share,
Till, from Mount Pisgah's lofty height,
I view my home, and take my flight:
This robe of flesh I'll drop, and rise
To seize the everlasting prize;
And shout, while passing through the air,
Farewell, farewell, sweet hour of prayer.

19. Blest Be the Tie That Binds

JOHN FAWCETT

HANS G. NAGELI
arr. by John W. Schaum

Andantino

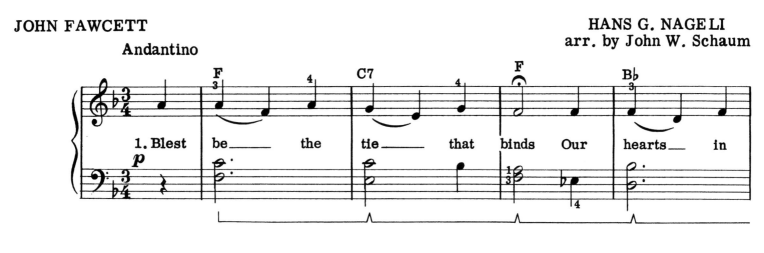

1. Blest be____ the tie____ that binds Our hearts____ in

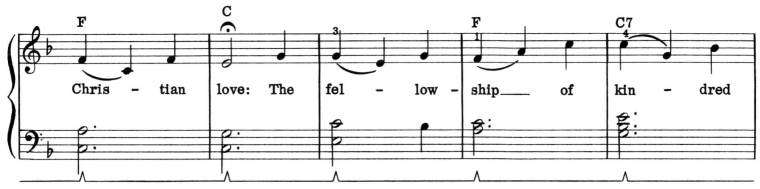

Chris - tian love: The fel - low - ship____ of kin - dred

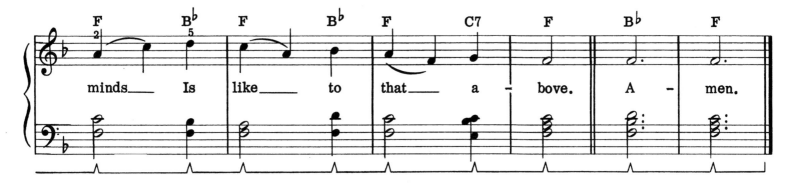

minds____ Is like____ to that____ a - bove. A - men.

2. Before our Father's throne
   We pour our ardent pray'rs;
   Our fears, our hopes, our aims are one,
   Our comforts and our cares.

3. We share each other's woes,
   Each other's burdens bear;
   And often for each other flows
   The sympathizing tear.

4. When we are called to part
   It gives us inward pain;
   But we shall still be joined in heart,
   And hope to meet again.

5. From sorrow, toil, and pain,
   And sin, we shall be free;
   And perfect love and friendship reign
   Through all eternity.

20. Abide With Me

H. F. LYTE

W. H. MONK
arr. by John W. Schaum

Lento

1. A - bide with me: fast falls the e - ven - tide;
The dark - ness deep - ens; Lord with me a - bide:
When oth - er help - ers fail, and com - forts flee,
Help of the help-less, O a - bide with me! A - men.

2. Swift to its close ebbs out life's little day;
   Earth's joys grow dim, its glories pass away;
   Change and decay in all around I see:
   O Thou who changest not, abide with me!

3. I need Thy presence every passing hour:
   What but Thy grace can foil the tempter's power?
   Who like Thyself my guide and stay can be?
   Through cloud and sunshine, O abide with me!

4. Hold Thou Thy word before my closing eyes;
   Shine through the gloom, and point me to the skies:
   Heaven's morning breaks, and earth's vain shadows flee
   In life, in death, O Lord, abide with me!

Schaum Hymn and Gospel Sing-Along Lyric Sheet

Series H and G

1. ALL HAIL THE POWER OF JESUS' NAME
All hail the power of Jesus' name!
Let angels prostrate fall;
Bring forth the royal diadem,
And crown Him Lord of all;
Bring forth the royal diadem,
And crown Him Lord of all

Ye chosen seed of Israel's race,
Ye ransomed from the fall,
Hail Him who saves you by His grace,
And crown Him Lord of all;
Hail Him who saves you by His Grace
And crown Him Lord of all!

Let every kindred, every tribe,
On this terrestrial ball,
To Him all majesty ascribe,
And crown Him Lord of all;
To Him all majesty ascribe,
And crown Him Lord of all!

O that with yonder sacred throng
We at His feet may fall
We'll join the everlasting song,
And crown Him Lord of all;
We'll join the everlasting song,
And crown Him Lord of all!

2. WHAT A FRIEND WE HAVE IN JESUS
What a Friend we have in Jesus,
All our sins and griefs to bear!
What a privilege to carry
Ev'rything to God in pray'r!
O what peace we often forfeit,
O what needless pain we bear,
All because we do not carry
Ev'rything to God in pray'r!

Have we trials and temptations?
Is there trouble anywhere?
We should never be discouraged,
Take it to the Lord in pray'r.
Can we find a friend so faithful
Who will all our sorrows share?
Jesus knows our ev'ry weakness,
Take it to the Lord in pray'r.

Are we weak and heavy laden,
Cumbered with a load of care?
Precious Saviour, still our refuge,
Take it to the Lord in pray'r.
Do thy friends despise, forsake thee?
Take it to the Lord in pray'r;
In His arms He'll take and shield thee,
Thou will find a solace there.

3. ROCK OF AGES
Rock of Ages, cleft for me,
Let me hide myself in Thee;
Let the water and the blood,
From Thy riven side which flowed,
Be of sin the double cure,
Save me from its guilt and pow'r.

Not the labor of my hands
Can fulfill Thy law's demands;
Could my zeal no respite know,
Could my tears forever flow,
All for sin could not atone;
Thou must save, and Thou alone.

Nothing in my hand I bring,
Simply to Thy cross I cling;
Naked, come to Thee for dress;
Helpless, look to Thee for grace;
Foul, I to the fountain fly,
Wash me, Savior, or I die.

While I draw this fleeting breath,
When mine eyes shall close in death,
When I soar to worlds unknown,
See Thee on Thy judgment throne,
Rock of Ages, cleft for me,
Let me hide myself in Thee.

4. A MIGHTY FORTRESS IS OUR GOD
A mighty fortress is our God,
A bulwark never failing;
Our helper He, amid the flood
Of mortal ills prevailing,
For still our ancient foe
Doth seek to work us woe;
His craft and power are great,
And, armed with cruel hate,
On earth is not his equal.

Did we in our own strength confide,
Our striving would be losing,

Were not the right Man on our side,
The Man of God's own choosing.
Dost ask who that may be?
Christ Jesus, it is He;
Lord Sabaoth is His name,
From age to age the same,
And He must win the battle.

And though this world, with devils filled,
Should threaten to undo us,
We will not fear, for God hath willed
His truth to triumph through us.
The prince of darkness grim —
We tremble not for him;
His rage we can endure,
For lo! his doom is sure:
One little word shall fell him.

That word above all earthly powers —
No thanks to them — abideth;
The Spirit and the gifts are ours
Thro' Him who with us sideth.
Let goods and kindred go,
This mortal life also;
The body they may kill;
God's truth abideth still,
His kingdom is forever.

5. ONWARD, CHRISTIAN SOLDIERS
Onward, Christian Soldiers!
Marching as to war,
With the cross of Jesus
Going on before;
Christ, the royal Master,
Leads against the foe;
Forward into battle,
See, His banners go!

Refrain:

Onward, Christian soldiers,
Marching as to war,
With the cross of Jesus
Going on before!

Like a mighty army
Moves the Church of God;
Brothers, we are treading
Where the saints have trod;
We are not divided;
All one body we,
One in hope and doctrine,
One in charity. Refrain

Crowns and thrones may perish,
Kingdoms rise and wane,
But the Church of Jesus
Constant will remain.
Gates of hell can never
'Gainst that Church prevail;
We have Christ's own promise,
And that cannot fail. Refrain

Onward, then, ye people,
Join our happy throng,
Blend with ours your voices
In the triumph song;
Glory, laud, and honor,
Unto Christ the King:
This thro' countless ages
Men and angels sing. Refrain

6. HOLY, HOLY, HOLY, LORD GOD ALMIGHTY
Holy, Holy, Holy, Lord God Almighty!
Early in the morning our song shall rise to
  Thee;
Holy, Holy, Holy! Merciful and Mighty!
God in Three Persons, blessed Trinity!

Holy, Holy, Holy! All the saints adore Thee,
Casting down their golden crowns around the
  glassy sea;
Cherubim and seraphim falling down before
  Thee,
Who wert, and art, and evermore shalt be.

Holy, Holy, Holy. Tho' the darkness hide
  Thee,
Tho' the eye of sinful man Thy glory may
  not see,
Only Thou art holy; there is none beside
  Thee
Perfect in pow'r, in love, in purity.

Holy, Holy, Holy, Lord God Almighty!
All Thy works shall praise Thy name in
  earth, and sky, and sea;
Holy, Holy, Holy! Merciful and Mighty!
God in Three Persons, blessed Trinity!

7. FAIREST LORD JESUS
Fairest Lord Jesus,
Ruler of all nature,
O Thou of God and man the Son,
Thee will I cherish,
Thee will I honor,
Thou my soul's glory, joy, and crown.

Fair are the meadows,
Fairer still the woodlands,
Robed in the blooming garb of spring;
Jesus is fairer,
Jesus is purer,
Who makes the woeful heart to sing.

Fair is the sunshine,
Fairer still the moonlight,
And all the twinkling, starry host;
Jesus shines brighter,
Jesus shines purer,
Than all the angels heaven can boast.

8. NEARER, MY GOD TO THEE
Nearer, my God, to Thee,
Nearer to Thee!
E'en though it be a cross
That raiseth me;
Still all my song shall be,
Nearer, my God, to Thee,
Nearer, my God, to Thee,
Nearer to Thee!

Though like the wanderer,
The sun gone down,
Darkness be over me,
My rest a stone;
Yet in my dreams I'd be
Nearer, my God, to Thee,
Nearer, my God, to Thee,
Nearer to Thee!

There let the way appear,
Steps unto heaven:
All that Thou sendest me,
In mercy given:
Angels to beckon me
Nearer, my God, to Thee,
Nearer, my God, to Thee,
Nearer to Thee!

Then with my waking thoughts
Bright with Thy praise,
Out of my stony griefs
Bethel I'll raise;
So by my woes to be
Nearer, my God, to Thee,
Nearer, my God, to Thee,
Nearer to Thee!

Or if on joyful wing,
Cleaving the sky,
Sun, moon, and stars forgot,
Upward I fly,
Still all my song shall be,
Nearer, my God, to Thee,
Nearer, my God, to Thee,
Nearer to Thee!

9. FACE TO FACE
Face to face with Christ my Saviour,
Face to face — what will it be —
When with rapture I behold Him,
Jesus Christ who died for me?

Refrain:
Face to face I shall behold Him,
Far beyond the starry sky;
Face to face in all His glory,
I shall see him by and by.

Only faintly now I see Him,
With the darkling veil between;
But a blessed day is coming,
When His glory shall be seen. Refrain

What rejoicing in His presence,
When are banished grief and pain;
When the crooked ways are straightened,
And the dark things shall be plain. Refrain

Face to face! O blissful moment!
Face to face — to see and know;
Face to face with my Redeemer,
Jesus Christ who loves me so. Refrain

10. SOFTLY AND TENDERLY
Softly and tenderly Jesus is calling,
Calling for you and for me;
See, on the portals He's waiting and
  watching,
Watching for you and for me.

Refrain:
Come home, (Come home,) Come home;
  (Come home,)
Ye who are weary, come home;
Earnestly, tenderly, Jesus is calling,
Calling, O sinner, come home!

Why should we tarry when Jesus is pleading,
Pleading for you and for me?
Why should we linger and heed not His
  mercies,
Mercies for you and for me? Refrain

Time is now fleeting, the moments are
  passing,
Passing from you and from me;
Shadows are gathering, death-beds are
  coming,
Coming for you and for me. Refrain

Oh! for the wonderful love He has promised,
Promised for you and for me;
Tho' we have sinned, He has mercy and
  pardon,
Pardon for you and for me. Refrain

11. AMAZING GRACE
Amazing grace! how sweet the sound,
That saved a wretch like me!
I once was lost, but now am found,
Was blind, but now I see.

'Twas grace that taught my heart to fear,
And grace my fears relieved;
How precious did that grace appear
The hour I first believed!

Thru many dangers, toils and snares,
I have already come;
'Tis grace hath bro't me safe thus far
And grace will lead me home.

When we've been there ten thousand years,
Bright shining as the sun,
We've no less days to sing God's praise
Than when we first begun.

12. I LOVE TO TELL THE STORY
I love to tell the story
Of unseen things above,
Of Jesus and His glory,
Of Jesus and His love.
I love to tell the story,
Because I know 'tis true;
It satisfies my longings
As nothing else can do.

Refrain:
I love to tell the story,
'Twill be my theme in glory
To tell the old, old story
Of Jesus and His love.

I love to tell the story,
More wonderful it seems
Than all the golden fancies
Of all our golden dreams.
I love to tell the story,
It did so much for me;
And that is just the reason
I tell it now to thee. Refrain

I love to tell the story,
'Tis pleasant to repeat
What seems, each time I tell it,
More wonderfully sweet.
I love to tell the story,
For some have never heard
The message of salvation
From God's own holy word. Refrain

I love to tell the story,
For those who know it best
Seem hungering and thirsting
To hear it like the rest.
And when, in scenes of glory,
I sing the new, new song,
'Twill be the old, old story
That I have loved so long. Refrain

13. O THAT WILL BE GLORY
When all my labors and trials are o'er,
And I am safe on that beautiful shore,
Just to be near the dear Lord I adore,
Will thro' the ages be glory for me.

Refrain:
O that will be glory for me,
Glory for me, glory for me;
When by His grace I shall look on His face,
That will be glory, be glory for me.

When, by the gift of His infinite grace,
I am accorded in heaven a place,
Just to be there and to look on His face,
Will thro' the ages be glory for me. Refrain

Friends will be there I have loved long ago;
Joy like a river around me will flow;
Yet, just a smile from my Savior, I know,
Will thro' the ages be glory for me. Refrain

14. JESUS, LOVER OF MY SOUL
Jesus, Lover of my soul,
Let me to Thy bosom fly,
While the nearer waters roll,
While the tempest still is high:
Hide me, O my Saviour, hide,
Till the storm of life is past;
Safe into the haven guide;
O receive my soul at last!

Other refuge have I none;
Hangs my helpless soul on Thee;
Leave, ah! leave me not alone,
Still support and comfort me.
All my trust on Thee is stayed,
All my help from Thee I bring;
Cover my defenseless head
With the shadow of Thy wing.

Thou, O Christ, art all I want;
More than all in Thee I find:
Raise the fallen, cheer the faint,
Heal the sick, and lead the blind.
Just and holy is Thy name;
I am all unrighteousness;
False and full of sin I am,
Thou art full of truth and grace.

Plenteous grace with Thee is found,
Grace to cover all my sin;
Let the healing streams abound;
Make and keep me pure within.
Thou of life the Fountain art,
Freely let me take of Thee;
Spring Thou up within my heart.
Rise to all eternity.

15. BLESSED ASSURANCE
Blessed assurance, Jesus is mine!
O what a foretaste of glory divine!
Heir of salvation, purchase of God,
Born of His Spirit, washed in His blood.

Refrain:
This is my story, this is my song,
Praising my Saviour all the day long;
This is my story, this is my song,
Praising my Saviour all the day long.

Perfect submission, perfect delight,
Visions of rapture now burst on my sight!
Angels descending, bring from above
Echoes of mercy, whispers of love. Refrain

Perfect submission, all is at rest,
I in my Saviour am happy and blest;
Watching and waiting, looking above,
Filled with His goodness, lost in His love.
Refrain

16. HE LEADETH ME
He leadeth me! O blessed tho't!
O words with heav'nly comfort fraught!
Whate'er I do, where'er I be,
Still 'tis God's hand that leadeth me.

Refrain:
He leadeth me, He leadeth me,
By His own hand He leadeth me:
His faithful follower I would be,
For by His hand He leadeth me.

Sometimes 'mid scenes of deepest gloom,
Sometimes where Eden's bowers bloom,
By waters still, o'er troubled sea,
Still 'tis my God that leadeth me! Refrain

Lord, I would clasp Thy hand in mine,
Nor ever murmur nor repine,
Content, whatever lot I see,
Since 'tis my God that leadeth me! Refrain

And when my task on earth is done,
When, by Thy grace, the victry's won,
E'en death's cold wave I will not flee,
Since God thro' Jordan leadeth me. Refrain

17. FAITH OF OUR FATHERS
Faith of our fathers! living still
In spite of dungeon, fire and sword,
O how our hearts beat high with joy

Whene'er we hear that glorious word!
Faith of our fathers! holy faith!
We will be true to thee till death!

Our fathers, chained in prisons dark,
Were still in heart and conscience free:
How sweet would be their children's fate,
If they, like them, could die for thee!
Faith of our fathers! holy faith!
We will be true to thee till death!

Faith of our fathers, God's great power
Shall win all nations unto thee,
And through the truth that comes from God
Mankind shall then indeed be free.
Faith of our fathers, holy faith,
We will be true to thee till death.

Faith of our fathers! we will love
Both friend and foe in all our strife:
And preach thee, too, as love knows how,
By kindly words and virtuous life:
Faith of our fathers! holy faith!
We will be true to thee till death!

18. SWEET HOUR OF PRAYER
Sweet hour of prayer! sweet hour of prayer!
That calls me from a world of care,
And bids me at my Father's throne
Make all my wants and wishes known;
In seasons of distress and grief,
My soul has often found relief,
And oft escaped the tempter's snare
By thy return, sweet hour of prayer.

Sweet hour of prayer! sweet hour of prayer!
Thy wings shall my petition bear
To Him whose truth and faithfulness
Engage the waiting soul to bless;
And since He bids me seek His face,
Believe His Word and trust His grace,
I'll cast on Him my every care,
And wait for thee, sweet hour of prayer.

Sweet hour of prayer! sweet hour of prayer!
May I thy consolation share,
Till, from Mount Pisgah's lofty height,
I view my home, and take my flight:
This robe of flesh I'll drop, and rise
To seize the everlasting prize;
And shout, while passing through the air,
Farewell, farewell, sweet hour of prayer.

19. BLEST BE THE TIE THAT BINDS
Blest be the tie that binds
Our hearts in Christian love;
The fellowship of kindred minds
Is like to that above.

Before our Father's throne
We pour our ardent pray'rs;
Our fears, our hopes, our aims are one,
Our comforts and our cares.

We share each other's woes,
Each other's burdens bear;
And often for each other flows
The sympathizing tear.

When we are called to part
It gives us inward pain;
But we shall still be joined in heart,
And hope to meet again.

From sorrow, toil, and pain,
And sin, we shall be free;
And perfect love and friendship reign
Through all eternity.

20. ABIDE WITH ME
Abide with me: fast falls the eventide;
The darkness deepens; Lord, with me abide:
When other helpers fail, and comforts flee,
Help of the helpless, O abide with me!

Swift to its close ebbs out life's little day;
Earth's joys grow dim, its glories pass away;
Change and decay in all around I see;
O Thou who changest not, abide with me!

I need Thy presence every passing hour:
What but Thy grace can foil the tempter's
  power?
Who like Thyself my guide and stay can be?
Through cloud and sunshine, O abide with me!

Hold Thou Thy word before my closing eyes;
Shine through the gloom, and point me to
  the skies:
Heaven's morning breaks, and earth's vain
  shadows flee
In life, in death, O Lord, abide with me!

Schaum Hymn and Gospel Sing-Along Lyric Sheet

Series H and G

1. **ALL HAIL THE POWER OF JESUS' NAME**
All hail the power of Jesus' name!
Let angels prostrate fall;
Bring forth the royal diadem,
And crown Him Lord of all;
Bring forth the royal diadem,
And crown Him Lord of all

Ye chosen seed of Israel's race,
Ye ransomed from the fall,
Hail Him who saves you by His grace,
And crown Him Lord of all;
Hail Him who saves you by His Grace
And crown Him Lord of all!

Let every kindred, every tribe,
On this terrestrial ball,
To Him all majesty ascribe,
And crown Him Lord of all;
To Him all majesty ascribe,
And crown Him Lord of all!

O that with yonder sacred throng
We at His feet may fall
We'll join the everlasting song,
And crown Him Lord of all;
We'll join the everlasting song,
And crown Him Lord of all!

2. **WHAT A FRIEND WE HAVE IN JESUS**
What a Friend we have in Jesus,
All our sins and griefs to bear!
What a privilege to carry
Ev'rything to God in pray'r!
O what peace we often forfeit,
O what needless pain we bear,
All because we do not carry
Ev'rything to God in pray'r!

Have we trials and temptations?
Is there trouble anywhere?
We should never be discouraged,
Take it to the Lord in pray'r.
Can we find a friend so faithful
Who will all our sorrows share?
Jesus knows our ev'ry weakness,
Take it to the Lord in pray'r.

Are we weak and heavy laden,
Cumbered with a load of care?
Precious Saviour, still our refuge,
Take it to the Lord in pray'r.
Do thy friends despise, forsake thee?
Take it to the Lord in pray'r;
In His arms He'll take and shield thee,
Thou will find a solace there.

3. **ROCK OF AGES**
Rock of Ages, cleft for me,
Let me hide myself in Thee;
Let the water and the blood,
From Thy riven side which flowed,
Be of sin the double cure,
Save me from its guilt and pow'r.

Not the labor of my hands
Can fulfill Thy law's demands;
Could my zeal no respite know,
Could my tears forever flow,
All for sin could not atone;
Thou must save, and Thou alone.

Nothing in my hand I bring,
Simply to Thy cross I cling;
Naked, come to Thee for dress,
Helpless, look to Thee for grace;
Foul, I to the fountain fly,
Wash me, Savior, or I die.

While I draw this fleeting breath,
When mine eyes shall close in death,
When I soar to worlds unknown,
See Thee on Thy judgment throne,
Rock of Ages, cleft for me,
Let me hide myself in Thee.

4. **A MIGHTY FORTRESS IS OUR GOD**
A mighty fortress is our God,
A bulwark never failing;
Our helper He, amid the flood
Of mortal ills prevailing,
For still our ancient foe
Doth seek to work us woe;
His craft and power are great,
And, armed with cruel hate,
On earth is not his equal.

Did we in our own strength confide,
Our striving would be losing,

Were not the right Man on our side,
The Man of God's own choosing.
Dost ask who that may be?
Christ Jesus, it is He;
Lord Sabaoth is His name,
From age to age the same,
And He must win the battle.

And though this world, with devils filled,
Should threaten to undo us,
We will not fear, for God hath willed
His truth to triumph through us.
The prince of darkness grim —
We tremble not for him;
His rage we can endure,
For lo! his doom is sure:
One little word shall fell him.

That word above all earthly powers —
No thanks to them — abideth;
The Spirit and the gifts are ours
Thro' Him who with us sideth.
Let goods and kindred go,
This mortal life also;
The body they may kill;
God's truth abideth still,
His kingdom is forever.

5. **ONWARD, CHRISTIAN SOLDIERS**
Onward, Christian Soldiers!
Marching as to war,
With the cross of Jesus
Going on before;
Christ, the royal Master,
Leads against the foe;
Forward into battle,
See, His banners go!

Refrain:

Onward, Christian soldiers,
Marching as to war,
With the cross of Jesus
Going on before!

Like a mighty army
Moves the Church of God;
Brothers, we are treading
Where the saints have trod;
We are not divided;
All one body we,
One in hope and doctrine,
One in charity. Refrain

Crowns and thrones may perish,
Kingdoms rise and wane,
But the Church of Jesus
Constant will remain.
Gates of hell can never
'Gainst that Church prevail;
We have Christ's own promise,
And that cannot fail. Refrain

Onward, then, ye people,
Join our happy throng,
Blend with ours your voices
In the triumph song;
Glory, laud, and honor,
Unto Christ the King:
This thro' countless ages
Men and angels sing. Refrain

6. **HOLY, HOLY, HOLY, LORD GOD ALMIGHTY**
Holy, Holy, Holy, Lord God Almighty!
Early in the morning our song shall rise to
    Thee;
Holy, Holy, Holy! Merciful and Mighty!
God in Three Persons, blessed Trinity!

Holy, Holy, Holy! All the saints adore Thee,
Casting down their golden crowns around the
    glassy sea;
Cherubim and seraphim falling down before
    Thee,
Who wert, and art, and evermore shalt be.

Holy, Holy, Holy. Tho' the darkness hide
    Thee,
Tho' the eye of sinful man Thy glory may
    not see,
Only Thou art holy; there is none beside
    Thee
Perfect in pow'r, in love, in purity.

Holy, Holy, Holy, Lord God Almighty!
All Thy works shall praise Thy name in
    earth, and sky, and sea;
Holy, Holy, Holy! Merciful and Mighty!
God in Three Persons, blessed Trinity!

7. **FAIREST LORD JESUS**
Fairest Lord Jesus,
Ruler of all nature,
O Thou of God and man the Son,
Thee will I cherish,
Thee will I honor,
Thou my soul's glory, joy, and crown.

Fair are the meadows,
Fairer still the woodlands,
Robed in the blooming garb of spring;
Jesus is fairer,
Jesus is purer,
Who makes the woeful heart to sing.

Fair is the sunshine,
Fairer still the moonlight,
And all the twinkling, starry host;
Jesus shines brighter,
Jesus shines purer,
Than all the angels heaven can boast.

8. **NEARER, MY GOD TO THEE**
Nearer, my God, to Thee,
Nearer to Thee!
E'en though it be a cross
That raiseth me;
Still all my song shall be,
Nearer, my God, to Thee,
Nearer, my God, to Thee,
Nearer to Thee!

Though like the wanderer,
The sun gone down,
Darkness be over me,
My rest a stone;
Yet in my dreams I'd be
Nearer, my God, to Thee,
Nearer, my God, to Thee,
Nearer to Thee!

There let the way appear,
Steps unto heaven:
All that Thou sendest me,
In mercy given:
Angels to beckon me
Nearer, my God, to Thee,
Nearer, my God, to Thee,
Nearer to Thee!

Then with my waking thoughts
Bright with Thy praise,
Out of my stony griefs
Bethel I'll raise;
So by my woes to be
Nearer, my God, to Thee,
Nearer, my God, to Thee,
Nearer to Thee!

Or if on joyful wing,
Cleaving the sky,
Sun, moon, and stars forgot,
Upward I fly,
Still all my song shall be,
Nearer, my God, to Thee,
Nearer, my God, to Thee,
Nearer to Thee!

9. **FACE TO FACE**
Face to face with Christ my Saviour,
Face to face — what will it be —
When with rapture I behold Him,
Jesus Christ who died for me?

Refrain:
Face to face I shall behold Him,
Far beyond the starry sky;
Face to face in all His glory,
I shall see him by and by.

Only faintly now I see Him,
With the darkling veil between;
But a blessed day is coming,
When His glory shall be seen. Refrain

What rejoicing in His presence,
When are banished grief and pain;
When the crooked ways are straightened,
And the dark things shall be plain. Refrain

Face to face! O blissful moment!
Face to face — to see and know;
Face to face with my Redeemer,
Jesus Christ who loves me so. Refrain

10. **SOFTLY AND TENDERLY**
Softly and tenderly Jesus is calling,
Calling for you and for me;
See, on the portals He's waiting and
    watching,
Watching for you and for me.

Refrain:

Come home, (Come home,) Come home;
(Come home,)
Ye who are weary, come home;
Earnestly, tenderly, Jesus is calling,
Calling, O sinner, come home!

Why should we tarry when Jesus is pleading,
Pleading for you and for me?
Why should we linger and heed not His
  mercies,
Mercies for you and for me? Refrain

Time is now fleeting, the moments are
  passing,
Passing from you and from me;
Shadows are gathering, death-beds are
  coming,
Coming for you and for me. Refrain

Oh! for the wonderful love He has promised,
Promised for you and for me;
Tho' we have sinned, He has mercy and
  pardon,
Pardon for you and for me. Refrain

11. AMAZING GRACE
Amazing grace! how sweet the sound,
That saved a wretch like me!
I once was lost, but now am found,
Was blind, but now I see.

'Twas grace that taught my heart to fear,
And grace my fears relieved;
How precious did that grace appear
The hour I first believed!

Thru many dangers, toils and snares,
I have already come;
'Tis grace hath bro't me safe thus far
And grace will lead me home.

When we've been there ten thousand years,
Bright shining as the sun,
We've no less days to sing God's praise
Than when we first begun.

12. I LOVE TO TELL THE STORY
I love to tell the story
Of unseen things above,
Of Jesus and His glory,
Of Jesus and His love.
I love to tell the story,
Because I know 'tis true;
It satisfies my longings
As nothing else can do.

Refrain:

I love to tell the story,
'Twill be my theme in glory
To tell the old, old story
Of Jesus and His love.

I love to tell the story,
More wonderful it seems
Than all the golden fancies
Of all our golden dreams.
I love to tell the story,
It did so much for me;
And that is just the reason
I tell it now to thee. Refrain

I love to tell the story,
'Tis pleasant to repeat
What seems, each time I tell it,
More wonderfully sweet.
I love to tell the story,
For some have never heard
The message of salvation
From God's own holy word. Refrain

I love to tell the story,
For those who know it best
Seem hungering and thirsting
To hear it like the rest.
And when, in scenes of glory,
I sing the new, new song,
'Twill be the old, old story
That I have loved so long. Refrain

13. O THAT WILL BE GLORY
When all my labors and trials are o'er,
And I am safe on that beautiful shore,
Just to be near the dear Lord I adore,
Will thro' the ages be glory for me.

Refrain:

O that will be glory for me,
Glory for me, glory for me;
When by His grace I shall look on His face,
That will be glory, be glory for me.

When, by the gift of His infinite grace,
I am accorded in heaven a place,
Just to be there and to look on His face,
Will thro' the ages be glory for me. Refrain

Friends will be there I have loved long ago;
Joy like a river around me will flow;
Yet, just a smile from my Savior, I know,
Will thro' the ages be glory for me. Refrain

14. JESUS, LOVER OF MY SOUL
Jesus, Lover of my soul,
Let me to Thy bosom fly,
While the nearer waters roll,
While the tempest still is high:
Hide me, O my Saviour, hide,
Till the storm of life is past;
Safe into the haven guide;
O receive my soul at last!

Other refuge have I none;
Hangs my helpless soul on Thee;
Leave, ah! leave me not alone,
Still support and comfort me.
All my trust on Thee is stayed,
All my help from Thee I bring;
Cover my defenseless head
With the shadow of Thy wing.

Thou, O Christ, art all I want;
More than all in Thee I find:
Raise the fallen, cheer the faint,
Heal the sick, and lead the blind.
Just and holy is Thy name;
I am all unrighteousness;
False and full of sin I am,
Thou art full of truth and grace.

Plenteous grace with Thee is found,
Grace to cover all my sin;
Let the healing streams abound;
Make and keep me pure within.
Thou of life the Fountain art,
Freely let me take of Thee;
Spring Thou up within my heart.
Rise to all eternity.

15. BLESSED ASSURANCE
Blessed assurance, Jesus is mine!
O what a foretaste of glory divine!
Heir of salvation, purchase of God,
Born of His Spirit, washed in His blood.

Refrain:

This is my story, this is my song,
Praising my Saviour all the day long;
This is my story, this is my song,
Praising my Saviour all the day long.

Perfect submission, perfect delight,
Visions of rapture now burst on my sight!
Angels descending, bring from above
Echoes of mercy, whispers of love. Refrain

Perfect submission, all is at rest,
I in my Saviour am happy and blest;
Watching and waiting, looking above,
Filled with His goodness, lost in His love.
Refrain

16. HE LEADETH ME
He leadeth me! O blessed tho't!
O words with heav'nly comfort fraught!
Whate'er I do, where'er I be,
Still 'tis God's hand that leadeth me.

Refrain:
He leadeth me, He leadeth me,
By His own hand He leadeth me:
His faithful follower I would be,
For by His hand He leadeth me.

Sometimes 'mid scenes of deepest gloom,
Sometimes where Eden's bowers bloom,
By waters still, o'er troubled sea,
Still 'tis my God that leadeth me! Refrain

Lord, I would clasp Thy hand in mine,
Nor ever murmur nor repine,
Content, whatever lot I see,
Since 'tis my God that leadeth me! Refrain

And when my task on earth is done,
When, by Thy grace, the victry's won,
E'en death's cold wave I will not flee,
Since God thro' Jordan leadeth me. Refrain

17. FAITH OF OUR FATHERS
Faith of our fathers! living still
In spite of dungeon, fire and sword,
O how our hearts beat high with joy

Whene'er we hear that glorious word!
Faith of our fathers! holy faith!
We will be true to thee till death!

Our fathers, chained in prisons dark,
Were still in heart and conscience free:
How sweet would be their children's fate,
If they, like them, could die for thee!
Faith of our fathers! holy faith!
We will be true to thee till death!

Faith of our fathers, God's great power
Shall win all nations unto thee,
And through the truth that comes from God
Mankind shall then indeed be free.
Faith of our fathers, holy faith,
We will be true to thee till death.

Faith of our fathers! we will love
Both friend and foe in all our strife:
And preach thee, too, as love knows how,
By kindly words and virtuous life:
Faith of our fathers! holy faith!
We will be true to thee till death!

18. SWEET HOUR OF PRAYER
Sweet hour of prayer! sweet hour of prayer!
That calls me from a world of care,
And bids me at my Father's throne
Make all my wants and wishes known;
In seasons of distress and grief,
My soul has often found relief,
And oft escaped the tempter's snare
By thy return, sweet hour of prayer.

Sweet hour of prayer! sweet hour of prayer!
Thy wings shall my petition bear
To Him whose truth and faithfulness
Engage the waiting soul to bless;
And since He bids me seek His face,
Believe His Word and trust His grace,
I'll cast on Him my every care,
And wait for thee, sweet hour of prayer.

Sweet hour of prayer! sweet hour of prayer!
May I thy consolation share,
Till, from Mount Pisgah's lofty height,
I view my home, and take my flight:
This robe of flesh I'll drop, and rise
To seize the everlasting prize;
And shout, while passing through the air,
Farewell, farewell, sweet hour of prayer.

19. BLEST BE THE TIE THAT BINDS
Blest be the tie that binds
Our hearts in Christian love;
The fellowship of kindred minds
Is like to that above.

Before our Father's throne
We pour our ardent pray'rs;
Our fears, our hopes, our aims are one,
Our comforts and our cares.

We share each other's woes,
Each other's burdens bear;
And often for each other flows
The sympathizing tear.

When we are called to part
It gives us inward pain;
But we shall still be joined in heart,
And hope to meet again.

From sorrow, toil, and pain,
And sin, we shall be free;
And perfect love and friendship reign
Through all eternity.

20. ABIDE WITH ME
Abide with me: fast falls the eventide;
The darkness deepens; Lord, with me abide:
When other helpers fail, and comforts flee,
Help of the helpless, O abide with me!

Swift to its close ebbs out life's little day;
Earth's joys grow dim, its glories pass away;
Change and decay in all around I see:
O Thou who changest not, abide with me!

I need Thy presence every passing hour:
What but Thy grace can foil the tempter's
  power?
Who like Thyself my guide and stay can be?
Through cloud and sunshine, O abide with me!

Hold Thou Thy word before my closing eyes;
Shine through the gloom, and point me to
  the skies:
Heaven's morning breaks, and earth's vain
  shadows flee
In life, in death, O Lord, abide with me!

Schaum Hymn and Gospel Sing-Along Lyric Sheet

Series H and G

1. ALL HAIL THE POWER OF JESUS' NAME
All hail the power of Jesus' name!
Let angels prostrate fall;
Bring forth the royal diadem,
And crown Him Lord of all;
Bring forth the royal diadem,
And crown Him Lord of all

Ye chosen seed of Israel's race,
Ye ransomed from the fall,
Hail Him who saves you by His grace,
And crown Him Lord of all;
Hail Him who saves you by His Grace
And crown Him Lord of all!

Let every kindred, every tribe,
On this terrestrial ball,
To Him all majesty ascribe,
And crown Him Lord of all;
To Him all majesty ascribe,
And crown Him Lord of all!

O that with yonder sacred throng
We at His feet may fall
We'll join the everlasting song,
And crown Him Lord of all;
We'll join the everlasting song,
And crown Him Lord of all!

2. WHAT A FRIEND WE HAVE IN JESUS
What a Friend we have in Jesus,
All our sins and griefs to bear!
What a privilege to carry
Ev'rything to God in pray'r!
O what peace we often forfeit,
O what needless pain we bear,
All because we do not carry
Ev'rything to God in pray'r!

Have we trials and temptations?
Is there trouble anywhere?
We should never be discouraged,
Take it to the Lord in pray'r.
Can we find a friend so faithful
Who will all our sorrows share?
Jesus knows our ev'ry weakness,
Take it to the Lord in pray'r.

Are we weak and heavy laden,
Cumbered with a load of care?
Precious Saviour, still our refuge,
Take it to the Lord in pray'r.
Do thy friends despise, forsake thee?
Take it to the Lord in pray'r;
In His arms He'll take and shield thee,
Thou will find a solace there.

3. ROCK OF AGES
Rock of Ages, cleft for me,
Let me hide myself in Thee;
Let the water and the blood,
From Thy riven side which flowed,
Be of sin the double cure,
Save me from its guilt and pow'r.

Not the labor of my hands
Can fulfill Thy law's demands;
Could my zeal no respite know,
Could my tears forever flow,
All for sin could not atone;
Thou must save, and Thou alone.

Nothing in my hand I bring,
Simply to Thy cross I cling;
Naked, come to Thee for dress;
Helpless, look to Thee for grace;
Foul, I to the fountain fly,
Wash me, Savior, or I die.

While I draw this fleeting breath,
When mine eyes shall close in death,
When I soar to worlds unknown,
See Thee on Thy judgment throne,
Rock of Ages, cleft for me,
Let me hide myself in Thee.

4. A MIGHTY FORTRESS IS OUR GOD
A mighty fortress is our God,
A bulwark never failing;
Our helper He, amid the flood
Of mortal ills prevailing,
For still our ancient foe
Doth seek to work us woe;
His craft and power are great,
And, armed with cruel hate,
On earth is not his equal.

Did we in our own strength confide,
Our striving would be losing,

Were not the right Man on our side,
The Man of God's own choosing.
Dost ask who that may be?
Christ Jesus, it is He;
Lord Sabaoth is His name,
From age to age the same,
And He must win the battle.

And though this world, with devils filled,
Should threaten to undo us,
We will not fear, for God hath willed
His truth to triumph through us.
The prince of darkness grim —
We tremble not for him;
His rage we can endure,
For lo! his doom is sure:
One little word shall fell him.

That word above all earthly powers —
No thanks to them — abideth;
The Spirit and the gifts are ours
Thro' Him who with us sideth.
Let goods and kindred go,
This mortal life also;
The body they may kill;
God's truth abideth still,
His kingdom is forever.

5. ONWARD, CHRISTIAN SOLDIERS
Onward, Christian Soldiers!
Marching as to war,
With the cross of Jesus
Going on before;
Christ, the royal Master,
Leads against the foe;
Forward into battle,
See, His banners go!

Refrain:

Onward, Christian soldiers,
Marching as to war,
With the cross of Jesus
Going on before!

Like a mighty army
Moves the Church of God;
Brothers, we are treading
Where the saints have trod;
We are not divided;
All one body we,
One in hope and doctrine,
One in charity. Refrain

Crowns and thrones may perish,
Kingdoms rise and wane,
But the Church of Jesus
Constant will remain.
Gates of hell can never
'Gainst that Church prevail;
We have Christ's own promise,
And that cannot fail. Refrain

Onward, then, ye people,
Join our happy throng,
Blend with ours your voices
In the triumph song;
Glory, laud, and honor,
Unto Christ the King:
This thro' countless ages
Men and angels sing. Refrain

6. HOLY, HOLY, HOLY, LORD GOD ALMIGHTY
Holy, Holy, Holy, Lord God Almighty!
Early in the morning our song shall rise to Thee;
Holy, Holy, Holy! Merciful and Mighty!
God in Three Persons, blessed Trinity!

Holy, Holy, Holy! All the saints adore Thee,
Casting down their golden crowns around the glassy sea;
Cherubim and seraphim falling down before Thee,
Who wert, and art, and evermore shalt be.

Holy, Holy, Holy. Tho' the darkness hide Thee,
Tho' the eye of sinful man Thy glory may not see,
Only Thou art holy; there is none beside Thee
Perfect in pow'r, in love, in purity.

Holy, Holy, Holy, Lord God Almighty!
All Thy works shall praise Thy name in earth, and sky, and sea;
Holy, Holy, Holy! Merciful and Mighty!
God in Three Persons, blessed Trinity!

7. FAIREST LORD JESUS
Fairest Lord Jesus,
Ruler of all nature,
O Thou of God and man the Son,
Thee will I cherish,
Thee will I honor,
Thou my soul's glory, joy, and crown.

Fair are the meadows,
Fairer still the woodlands,
Robed in the blooming garb of spring;
Jesus is fairer,
Jesus is purer,
Who makes the woeful heart to sing.

Fair is the sunshine,
Fairer still the moonlight,
And all the twinkling, starry host;
Jesus shines brighter,
Jesus shines purer,
Than all the angels heaven can boast.

8. NEARER, MY GOD TO THEE
Nearer, my God, to Thee,
Nearer to Thee!
E'en though it be a cross
That raiseth me;
Still all my song shall be,
Nearer, my God, to Thee,
Nearer, my God, to Thee,
Nearer to Thee!

Though like the wanderer,
The sun gone down,
Darkness be over me,
My rest a stone;
Yet in my dreams I'd be
Nearer, my God, to Thee,
Nearer, my God, to Thee,
Nearer to Thee!

There let the way appear,
Steps unto heaven:
All that Thou sendest me,
In mercy given:
Angels to beckon me
Nearer, my God, to Thee,
Nearer, my God, to Thee,
Nearer to Thee!

Then with my waking thoughts
Bright with Thy praise,
Out of my stony griefs
Bethel I'll raise;
So by my woes to be
Nearer, my God, to Thee,
Nearer, my God, to Thee,
Nearer to Thee!

Or if on joyful wing,
Cleaving the sky,
Sun, moon, and stars forgot,
Upward I fly,
Still all my song shall be,
Nearer, my God, to Thee,
Nearer, my God, to Thee,
Nearer to Thee!

9. FACE TO FACE
Face to face with Christ my Saviour,
Face to face — what will it be —
When with rapture I behold Him,
Jesus Christ who died for me?

Refrain:
Face to face I shall behold Him,
Far beyond the starry sky;
Face to face in all His glory,
I shall see him by and by.

Only faintly now I see Him,
With the darkling veil between;
But a blessed day is coming,
When His glory shall be seen. Refrain

What rejoicing in His presence,
When are banished grief and pain;
When the crooked ways are straightened,
And the dark things shall be plain. Refrain

Face to face! O blissful moment!
Face to face — to see and know;
Face to face with my Redeemer,
Jesus Christ who loves me so. Refrain

10. SOFTLY AND TENDERLY
Softly and tenderly Jesus is calling,
Calling for you and for me;
See, on the portals He's waiting and watching,
Watching for you and for me.

Refrain:

Come home, (Come home,) Come home;
(Come home,)
Ye who are weary, come home;
Earnestly, tenderly, Jesus is calling,
Calling, O sinner, come home!

Why should we tarry when Jesus is pleading,
Pleading for you and for me?
Why should we linger and heed not His
mercies,
Mercies for you and for me? Refrain

Time is now fleeting, the moments are
passing,
Passing from you and from me;
Shadows are gathering, death-beds are
coming,
Coming for you and for me. Refrain

Oh! for the wonderful love He has promised,
Promised for you and for me;
Tho' we have sinned, He has mercy and
pardon,
Pardon for you and for me. Refrain

11. AMAZING GRACE
Amazing grace! how sweet the sound,
That saved a wretch like me!
I once was lost, but now am found,
Was blind, but now I see.

'Twas grace that taught my heart to fear,
And grace my fears relieved;
How precious did that grace appear
The hour I first believed!

Thru many dangers, toils and snares,
I have already come;
'Tis grace hath bro't me safe thus far
And grace will lead me home.

When we've been there ten thousand years,
Bright shining as the sun,
We've no less days to sing God's praise
Than when we first begun.

12. I LOVE TO TELL THE STORY
I love to tell the story
Of unseen things above,
Of Jesus and His glory,
Of Jesus and His love.
I love to tell the story,
Because I know 'tis true;
It satisfies my longings
As nothing else can do.

Refrain:

I love to tell the story,
'Twill be my theme in glory
To tell the old, old story
Of Jesus and His love.

I love to tell the story,
More wonderful it seems
Than all the golden fancies
Of all our golden dreams.
I love to tell the story,
It did so much for me;
And that is just the reason
I tell it now to thee. Refrain

I love to tell the story,
'Tis pleasant to repeat
What seems, each time I tell it,
More wonderfully sweet.
I love to tell the story,
For some have never heard
The message of salvation
From God's own holy word. Refrain

I love to tell the story,
For those who know it best
Seem hungering and thirsting
To hear it like the rest.
And when, in scenes of glory,
I sing the new, new song,
'Twill be the old, old story
That I have loved so long. Refrain

13. O THAT WILL BE GLORY
When all my labors and trials are o'er,
And I am safe on that beautiful shore,
Just to be near the dear Lord I adore,
Will thro' the ages be glory for me.

Refrain:

O that will be glory for me,
Glory for me, glory for me;
When by His grace I shall look on His face,
That will be glory, be glory for me.

When, by the gift of His infinite grace,
I am accorded in heaven a place,
Just to be there and to look on His face,
Will thro' the ages be glory for me. Refrain

Friends will be there I have loved long ago;
Joy like a river around me will flow;
Yet, just a smile from my Savior, I know,
Will thro' the ages be glory for me. Refrain

14. JESUS, LOVER OF MY SOUL
Jesus, Lover of my soul,
Let me to Thy bosom fly,
While the nearer waters roll,
While the tempest still is high:
Hide me, O my Saviour, hide,
Till the storm of life is past;
Safe into the haven guide;
O receive my soul at last!

Other refuge have I none;
Hangs my helpless soul on Thee;
Leave, ah! leave me not alone,
Still support and comfort me.
All my trust on Thee is stayed,
All my help from Thee I bring;
Cover my defenseless head
With the shadow of Thy wing.

Thou, O Christ, art all I want;
More than all in Thee I find:
Raise the fallen, cheer the faint,
Heal the sick, and lead the blind.
Just and holy is Thy name;
I am all unrighteousness;
False and full of sin I am,
Thou art full of truth and grace.

Plenteous grace with Thee is found,
Grace to cover all my sin;
Let the healing streams abound;
Make and keep me pure within.
Thou of life the Fountain art,
Freely let me take of Thee;
Spring Thou up within my heart.
Rise to all eternity.

15. BLESSED ASSURANCE
Blessed assurance, Jesus is mine!
O what a foretaste of glory divine!
Heir of salvation, purchase of God,
Born of His Spirit, washed in His blood.

Refrain:

This is my story, this is my song,
Praising my Saviour all the day long;
This is my story, this is my song,
Praising my Saviour all the day long.

Perfect submission, perfect delight,
Visions of rapture now burst on my sight!
Angels descending, bring from above
Echoes of mercy, whispers of love. Refrain

Perfect submission, all is at rest,
I in my Saviour am happy and blest;
Watching and waiting, looking above,
Filled with His goodness, lost in His love.
Refrain

16. HE LEADETH ME
He leadeth me! O blessed tho't!
O words with heav'nly comfort fraught!
Whate'er I do, where'er I be,
Still 'tis God's hand that leadeth me.

Refrain:

He leadeth me, He leadeth me,
By His own hand He leadeth me:
His faithful follower I would be,
For by His hand He leadeth me.

Sometimes 'mid scenes of deepest gloom,
Sometimes where Eden's bowers bloom,
By waters still, o'er troubled sea,
Still 'tis my God that leadeth me! Refrain

Lord, I would clasp Thy hand in mine,
Nor ever murmur nor repine,
Content, whatever lot I see,
Since 'tis my God that leadeth me! Refrain

And when my task on earth is done,
When, by Thy grace, the victry's won,
E'en death's cold wave I will not flee,
Since God thro' Jordan leadeth me. Refrain

17. FAITH OF OUR FATHERS
Faith of our fathers! living still
In spite of dungeon, fire and sword,
O how our hearts beat high with joy

Whene'er we hear that glorious word!
Faith of our fathers! holy faith!
We will be true to thee till death!

Our fathers, chained in prisons dark,
Were still in heart and conscience free:
How sweet would be their children's fate,
If they, like them, could die for thee!
Faith of our fathers! holy faith!
We will be true to thee till death!

Faith of our fathers, God's great power
Shall win all nations unto thee,
And through the truth that comes from God
Mankind shall then indeed be free.
Faith of our fathers, holy faith,
We will be true to thee till death.

Faith of our fathers! we will love
Both friend and foe in all our strife:
And preach thee, too, as love knows how,
By kindly words and virtuous life:
Faith of our fathers! holy faith!
We will be true to thee till death!

18. SWEET HOUR OF PRAYER
Sweet hour of prayer! sweet hour of prayer!
That calls me from a world of care,
And bids me at my Father's throne
Make all my wants and wishes known;
In seasons of distress and grief,
My soul has often found relief,
And oft escaped the tempter's snare
By thy return, sweet hour of prayer.

Sweet hour of prayer! sweet hour of prayer!
Thy wings shall my petition bear
To Him whose truth and faithfulness
Engage the waiting soul to bless;
And since He bids me seek His face,
Believe His Word and trust His grace,
I'll cast on Him my every care,
And wait for thee, sweet hour of prayer.

Sweet hour of prayer! sweet hour of prayer!
May I thy consolation share,
Till, from Mount Pisgah's lofty height,
I view my home, and take my flight:
This robe of flesh I'll drop, and rise
To seize the everlasting prize;
And shout, while passing through the air,
Farewell, farewell, sweet hour of prayer.

19. BLEST BE THE TIE THAT BINDS
Blest be the tie that binds
Our hearts in Christian love;
The fellowship of kindred minds
Is like to that above.

Before our Father's throne
We pour our ardent pray'rs;
Our fears, our hopes, our aims are one,
Our comforts and our cares.

We share each other's woes,
Each other's burdens bear;
And often for each other flows
The sympathizing tear.

When we are called to part
It gives us inward pain;
But we shall still be joined in heart,
And hope to meet again.

From sorrow, toil, and pain,
And sin, we shall be free;
And perfect love and friendship reign
Through all eternity.

20. ABIDE WITH ME
Abide with me: fast falls the eventide;
The darkness deepens; Lord, with me abide:
When other helpers fail, and comforts flee,
Help of the helpless, O abide with me!

Swift to its close ebbs out life's little day;
Earth's joys grow dim, its glories pass away;
Change and decay in all around I see:
O Thou who changest not, abide with me!

I need Thy presence every passing hour:
What but Thy grace can foil the tempter's
power?
Who like Thyself my guide and stay can be?
Through cloud and sunshine, O abide with me!

Hold Thou Thy word before my closing eyes;
Shine through the gloom, and point me to
the skies:
Heaven's morning breaks, and earth's vain
shadows flee
In life, in death, O Lord, abide with me!

Schaum Hymn and Gospel Sing-Along Lyric Sheet

Series H and G

1. **ALL HAIL THE POWER OF JESUS' NAME**
All hail the power of Jesus' name!
Let angels prostrate fall;
Bring forth the royal diadem,
And crown Him Lord of all;
Bring forth the royal diadem,
And crown Him Lord of all

Ye chosen seed of Israel's race,
Ye ransomed from the fall,
Hail Him who saves you by His grace,
And crown Him Lord of all;
Hail Him who saves you by His Grace
And crown Him Lord of all!

Let every kindred, every tribe,
On this terrestrial ball,
To Him all majesty ascribe,
And crown Him Lord of all;
To Him all majesty ascribe,
And crown Him Lord of all!

O that with yonder sacred throng
We at His feet may fall
We'll join the everlasting song,
And crown Him Lord of all;
We'll join the everlasting song,
And crown Him Lord of all!

2. **WHAT A FRIEND WE HAVE IN JESUS**
What a Friend we have in Jesus,
All our sins and griefs to bear!
What a privilege to carry
Ev'rything to God in pray'r!
O what peace we often forfeit,
O what needless pain we bear,
All because we do not carry
Ev'rything to God in pray'r!

Have we trials and temptations?
Is there trouble anywhere?
We should never be discouraged,
Take it to the Lord in pray'r.
Can we find a friend so faithful
Who will all our sorrows share?
Jesus knows our ev'ry weakness,
Take it to the Lord in pray'r.

Are we weak and heavy laden,
Cumbered with a load of care?
Precious Saviour, still our refuge,
Take it to the Lord in pray'r.
Do thy friends despise, forsake thee?
Take it to the Lord in pray'r;
In His arms He'll take and shield thee,
Thou will find a solace there.

3. **ROCK OF AGES**
Rock of Ages, cleft for me,
Let me hide myself in Thee;
Let the water and the blood,
From Thy riven side which flowed,
Be of sin the double cure,
Save me from its guilt and pow'r.

Not the labor of my hands
Can fulfill Thy law's demands;
Could my zeal no respite know,
Could my tears forever flow,
All for sin could not atone;
Thou must save, and Thou alone.

Nothing in my hand I bring,
Simply to Thy cross I cling;
Naked, come to Thee for dress;
Helpless, look to Thee for grace;
Foul, I to the fountain fly,
Wash me, Savior, or I die.

While I draw this fleeting breath,
When mine eyes shall close in death,
When I soar to worlds unknown,
See Thee on Thy judgment throne,
Rock of Ages, cleft for me,
Let me hide myself in Thee.

4. **A MIGHTY FORTRESS IS OUR GOD**
A mighty fortress is our God,
A bulwark never failing;
Our helper He, amid the flood
Of mortal ills prevailing,
For still our ancient foe
Doth seek to work us woe;
His craft and power are great,
And, armed with cruel hate,
On earth is not his equal.

Did we in our own strength confide,
Our striving would be losing,

Were not the right Man on our side,
The Man of God's own choosing.
Dost ask who that may be?
Christ Jesus, it is He;
Lord Sabaoth is His name,
From age to age the same,
And He must win the battle.

And though this world, with devils filled,
Should threaten to undo us,
We will not fear, for God hath willed
His truth to triumph through us.
The prince of darkness grim —
We tremble not for him;
His rage we can endure,
For lo! his doom is sure:
One little word shall fell him.

That word above all earthly powers —
No thanks to them — abideth;
The Spirit and the gifts are ours
Thro' Him who with us sideth.
Let goods and kindred go,
This mortal life also;
The body they may kill;
God's truth abideth still,
His kingdom is forever.

5. **ONWARD, CHRISTIAN SOLDIERS**
Onward, Christian Soldiers!
Marching as to war,
With the cross of Jesus
Going on before;
Christ, the royal Master,
Leads against the foe;
Forward into battle,
See, His banners go!

Refrain:

Onward, Christian soldiers,
Marching as to war,
With the cross of Jesus
Going on before!

Like a mighty army
Moves the Church of God;
Brothers, we are treading
Where the saints have trod;
We are not divided;
All one body we,
One in hope and doctrine,
One in charity. Refrain

Crowns and thrones may perish,
Kingdoms rise and wane,
But the Church of Jesus
Constant will remain.
Gates of hell can never
'Gainst that Church prevail;
We have Christ's own promise,
And that cannot fail. Refrain

Onward, then, ye people,
Join our happy throng,
Blend with ours your voices
In the triumph song;
Glory, laud, and honor,
Unto Christ the King:
This thro' countless ages
Men and angels sing. Refrain

6. **HOLY, HOLY, HOLY, LORD GOD ALMIGHTY**
Holy, Holy, Holy, Lord God Almighty!
Early in the morning our song shall rise to
Thee;
Holy, Holy, Holy! Merciful and Mighty!
God in Three Persons, blessed Trinity!

Holy, Holy, Holy! All the saints adore Thee,
Casting down their golden crowns around the
glassy sea;
Cherubim and seraphim falling down before
Thee,
Who wert, and art, and evermore shalt be.

Holy, Holy, Holy. Tho' the darkness hide
Thee,
Tho' the eye of sinful man Thy glory may
not see,
Only Thou art holy; there is none beside
Thee
Perfect in pow'r, in love, in purity.

Holy, Holy, Holy, Lord God Almighty!
All Thy works shall praise Thy name in
earth, and sky, and sea;
Holy, Holy, Holy! Merciful and Mighty!
God in Three Persons, blessed Trinity!

7. **FAIREST LORD JESUS**
Fairest Lord Jesus,
Ruler of all nature,
O Thou of God and man the Son,
Thee will I cherish,
Thee will I honor,
Thou my soul's glory, joy, and crown.

Fair are the meadows,
Fairer still the woodlands,
Robed in the blooming garb of spring;
Jesus is fairer,
Jesus is purer,
Who makes the woeful heart to sing.

Fair is the sunshine,
Fairer still the moonlight,
And all the twinkling, starry host;
Jesus shines brighter,
Jesus shines purer,
Than all the angels heaven can boast.

8. **NEARER, MY GOD TO THEE**
Nearer, my God, to Thee,
Nearer to Thee!
E'en though it be a cross
That raiseth me;
Still all my song shall be,
Nearer, my God, to Thee,
Nearer, my God, to Thee,
Nearer to Thee!

Though like the wanderer,
The sun gone down,
Darkness be over me,
My rest a stone;
Yet in my dreams I'd be
Nearer, my God, to Thee,
Nearer, my God, to Thee,
Nearer to Thee!

There let the way appear,
Steps unto heaven;
All that Thou sendest me,
In mercy given;
Angels to beckon me
Nearer, my God, to Thee,
Nearer, my God, to Thee,
Nearer to Thee!

Then with my waking thoughts
Bright with Thy praise,
Out of my stony griefs
Bethel I'll raise;
So by my woes to be
Nearer, my God, to Thee,
Nearer, my God, to Thee,
Nearer to Thee!

Or if on joyful wing,
Cleaving the sky,
Sun, moon, and stars forgot,
Upward I fly,
Still all my song shall be,
Nearer, my God, to Thee,
Nearer, my God, to Thee,
Nearer to Thee!

9. **FACE TO FACE**
Face to face with Christ my Saviour,
Face to face — what will it be —
When with rapture I behold Him,
Jesus Christ who died for me?

Refrain:
Face to face I shall behold Him,
Far beyond the starry sky;
Face to face in all His glory,
I shall see him by and by.

Only faintly now I see Him,
With the darkling veil between;
But a blessed day is coming,
When His glory shall be seen. Refrain

What rejoicing in His presence,
When are banished grief and pain;
When the crooked ways are straightened,
And the dark things shall be plain. Refrain

Face to face! O blissful moment!
Face to face — to see and know;
Face to face with my Redeemer,
Jesus Christ who loves me so. Refrain

10. **SOFTLY AND TENDERLY**
Softly and tenderly Jesus is calling,
Calling for you and for me;
See, on the portals He's waiting and
watching,
Watching for you and for me.

Refrain:
Come home, (Come home,) Come home;
(Come home,)
Ye who are weary, come home;
Earnestly, tenderly, Jesus is calling,
Calling, O sinner, come home!

Why should we tarry when Jesus is pleading,
Pleading for you and for me?
Why should we linger and heed not His
mercies,
Mercies for you and for me? Refrain

Time is now fleeting, the moments are
passing,
Passing from you and from me;
Shadows are gathering, death-beds are
coming,
Coming for you and for me. Refrain

Oh! for the wonderful love He has promised,
Promised for you and for me;
Tho' we have sinned, He has mercy and
pardon,
Pardon for you and for me. Refrain

11. AMAZING GRACE
Amazing grace! how sweet the sound,
That saved a wretch like me!
I once was lost, but now am found,
Was blind, but now I see.

'Twas grace that taught my heart to fear,
And grace my fears relieved;
How precious did that grace appear
The hour I first believed!

Thru many dangers, toils and snares,
I have already come;
'Tis grace hath bro't me safe thus far
And grace will lead me home.

When we've been there ten thousand years,
Bright shining as the sun,
We've no less days to sing God's praise
Than when we first begun.

12. I LOVE TO TELL THE STORY
I love to tell the story
Of unseen things above,
Of Jesus and His glory,
Of Jesus and His love.
I love to tell the story,
Because I know 'tis true;
It satisfies my longings
As nothing else can do.

Refrain:
I love to tell the story,
'Twill be my theme in glory
To tell the old, old story
Of Jesus and His love.

I love to tell the story,
More wonderful it seems
Than all the golden fancies
Of all our golden dreams.
I love to tell the story,
It did so much for me;
And that is just the reason
I tell it now to thee. Refrain

I love to tell the story,
'Tis pleasant to repeat
What seems, each time I tell it,
More wonderfully sweet.
I love to tell the story,
For some have never heard
The message of salvation
From God's own holy word. Refrain

I love to tell the story,
For those who know it best
Seem hungering and thirsting
To hear it like the rest.
And when, in scenes of glory,
I sing the new, new song,
'Twill be the old, old story
That I have loved so long. Refrain

13. O THAT WILL BE GLORY
When all my labors and trials are o'er,
And I am safe on that beautiful shore,
Just to be near the dear Lord I adore,
Will thro' the ages be glory for me.

Refrain:
O that will be glory for me,
Glory for me, glory for me;
When by His grace I shall look on His face,
That will be glory, be glory for me.

When, by the gift of His infinite grace,
I am accorded in heaven a place,
Just to be there and to look on His face,
Will thro' the ages be glory for me. Refrain

Friends will be there I have loved long ago;
Joy like a river around me will flow;
Yet, just a smile from my Savior, I know,
Will thro' the ages be glory for me. Refrain

14. JESUS, LOVER OF MY SOUL
Jesus, Lover of my soul,
Let me to Thy bosom fly,
While the nearer waters roll,
While the tempest still is high:
Hide me, O my Saviour, hide,
Till the storm of life is past;
Safe into the haven guide;
O receive my soul at last!

Other refuge have I none;
Hangs my helpless soul on Thee;
Leave, ah! leave me not alone,
Still support and comfort me.
All my trust on Thee is stayed,
All my help from Thee I bring;
Cover my defenseless head
With the shadow of Thy wing.

Thou, O Christ, art all I want;
More than all in Thee I find:
Raise the fallen, cheer the faint,
Heal the sick, and lead the blind.
Just and holy is Thy name;
I am all unrighteousness;
False and full of sin I am,
Thou art full of truth and grace.

Plenteous grace with Thee is found,
Grace to cover all my sin;
Let the healing streams abound;
Make and keep me pure within.
Thou of life the Fountain art,
Freely let me take of Thee;
Spring Thou up within my heart.
Rise to all eternity.

15. BLESSED ASSURANCE
Blessed assurance, Jesus is mine!
O what a foretaste of glory divine!
Heir of salvation, purchase of God,
Born of His Spirit, washed in His blood.

Refrain:
This is my story, this is my song,
Praising my Saviour all the day long;
This is my story, this is my song,
Praising my Saviour all the day long.

Perfect submission, perfect delight,
Visions of rapture now burst on my sight!
Angels descending, bring from above
Echoes of mercy, whispers of love. Refrain

Perfect submission, all is at rest,
I in my Saviour am happy and blest;
Watching and waiting, looking above,
Filled with His goodness, lost in His love.
Refrain

16. HE LEADETH ME
He leadeth me! O blessed tho't!
O words with heav'nly comfort fraught!
Whate'er I do, where'er I be,
Still 'tis God's hand that leadeth me.

Refrain:
He leadeth me, He leadeth me,
By His own hand He leadeth me:
His faithful follower I would be,
For by His hand He leadeth me.

Sometimes 'mid scenes of deepest gloom,
Sometimes where Eden's bowers bloom,
By waters still, o'er troubled sea,
Still 'tis my God that leadeth me! Refrain

Lord, I would clasp Thy hand in mine,
Nor ever murmur nor repine,
Content, whatever lot I see,
Since 'tis my God that leadeth me! Refrain

And when my task on earth is done,
When, by Thy grace, the victry's won,
E'en death's cold wave I will not flee,
Since God thro' Jordan leadeth me. Refrain

17. FAITH OF OUR FATHERS
Faith of our fathers! living still
In spite of dungeon, fire and sword,
O how our hearts beat high with joy

Whene'er we hear that glorious word!
Faith of our fathers! holy faith!
We will be true to thee till death!

Our fathers, chained in prisons dark,
Were still in heart and conscience free:
How sweet would be their children's fate,
If they, like them, could die for thee!
Faith of our fathers! holy faith!
We will be true to thee till death!

Faith of our fathers, God's great power
Shall win all nations unto thee,
And through the truth that comes from God
Mankind shall then indeed be free.
Faith of our fathers, holy faith,
We will be true to thee till death.

Faith of our fathers! we will love
Both friend and foe in all our strife:
And preach thee, too, as love knows how,
By kindly words and virtuous life:
Faith of our fathers! holy faith!
We will be true to thee till death!

18. SWEET HOUR OF PRAYER
Sweet hour of prayer! sweet hour of prayer!
That calls me from a world of care,
And bids me at my Father's throne
Make all my wants and wishes known;
In seasons of distress and grief,
My soul has often found relief,
And oft escaped the tempter's snare
By thy return, sweet hour of prayer.

Sweet hour of prayer! sweet hour of prayer!
Thy wings shall my petition bear
To Him whose truth and faithfulness
Engage the waiting soul to bless;
And since He bids me seek His face,
Believe His Word and trust His grace,
I'll cast on Him my every care,
And wait for thee, sweet hour of prayer.

Sweet hour of prayer! sweet hour of prayer!
May I thy consolation share,
Till, from Mount Pisgah's lofty height,
I view my home, and take my flight:
This robe of flesh I'll drop, and rise
To seize the everlasting prize;
And shout, while passing through the air,
Farewell, farewell, sweet hour of prayer.

19. BLEST BE THE TIE THAT BINDS
Blest be the tie that binds
Our hearts in Christian love;
The fellowship of kindred minds
Is like to that above.

Before our Father's throne
We pour our ardent pray'rs;
Our fears, our hopes, our aims are one,
Our comforts and our cares.

We share each other's woes,
Each other's burdens bear;
And often for each other flows
The sympathizing tear.

When we are called to part
It gives us inward pain;
But we shall still be joined in heart,
And hope to meet again.

From sorrow, toil, and pain,
And sin, we shall be free;
And perfect love and friendship reign
Through all eternity.

20. ABIDE WITH ME
Abide with me: fast falls the eventide;
The darkness deepens; Lord, with me abide:
When other helpers fail, and comforts flee,
Help of the helpless, O abide with me!

Swift to its close ebbs out life's little day;
Earth's joys grow dim, its glories pass away;
Change and decay in all around I see:
O Thou who changest not, abide with me!

I need Thy presence every passing hour:
What but Thy grace can foil the tempter's
power?
Who like Thyself my guide and stay can be?
Through cloud and sunshine, O abide with me!

Hold Thou Thy word before my closing eyes;
Shine through the gloom, and point me to
the skies:
Heaven's morning breaks, and earth's vain
shadows flee
In life, in death, O Lord, abide with me!

Schaum Hymn and Gospel Sing-Along Lyric Sheet

Series H and G

1. **ALL HAIL THE POWER OF JESUS' NAME**
All hail the power of Jesus' name!
Let angels prostrate fall;
Bring forth the royal diadem,
And crown Him Lord of all;
Bring forth the royal diadem,
And crown Him Lord of all

Ye chosen seed of Israel's race,
Ye ransomed from the fall,
Hail Him who saves you by His grace,
And crown Him Lord of all;
Hail Him who saves you by His Grace
And crown Him Lord of all!

Let every kindred, every tribe,
On this terrestrial ball,
To Him all majesty ascribe,
And crown Him Lord of all;
To Him all majesty ascribe,
And crown Him Lord of all!

O that with yonder sacred throng
We at His feet may fall!
We'll join the everlasting song,
And crown Him Lord of all;
We'll join the everlasting song,
And crown Him Lord of all!

2. **WHAT A FRIEND WE HAVE IN JESUS**
What a Friend we have in Jesus,
All our sins and griefs to bear!
What a privilege to carry
Ev'rything to God in pray'r!
O what peace we often forfeit,
O what needless pain we bear,
All because we do not carry
Ev'rything to God in pray'r!

Have we trials and temptations?
Is there trouble anywhere?
We should never be discouraged,
Take it to the Lord in pray'r.
Can we find a friend so faithful
Who will all our sorrows share?
Jesus knows our ev'ry weakness,
Take it to the Lord in pray'r.

Are we weak and heavy laden,
Cumbered with a load of care?
Precious Saviour, still our refuge,
Take it to the Lord in pray'r.
Do thy friends despise, forsake thee?
Take it to the Lord in pray'r;
In His arms He'll take and shield thee,
Thou will find a solace there.

3. **ROCK OF AGES**
Rock of Ages, cleft for me,
Let me hide myself in Thee;
Let the water and the blood,
From Thy riven side which flowed,
Be of sin the double cure,
Save me from its guilt and pow'r.

Not the labor of my hands
Can fulfill Thy law's demands;
Could my zeal no respite know,
Could my tears forever flow,
All for sin could not atone;
Thou must save, and Thou alone.

Nothing in my hand I bring,
Simply to Thy cross I cling;
Naked, come to Thee for dress;
Helpless, look to Thee for grace;
Foul, I to the fountain fly,
Wash me, Savior, or I die.

While I draw this fleeting breath,
When mine eyes shall close in death,
When I soar to worlds unknown,
See Thee on Thy judgment throne,
Rock of Ages, cleft for me,
Let me hide myself in Thee.

4. **A MIGHTY FORTRESS IS OUR GOD**
A mighty fortress is our God,
A bulwark never failing;
Our helper He, amid the flood
Of mortal ills prevailing,
For still our ancient foe
Doth seek to work us woe;
His craft and power are great,
And, armed with cruel hate,
On earth is not his equal.

Did we in our own strength confide,
Our striving would be losing,

Were not the right Man on our side,
The Man of God's own choosing.
Dost ask who that may be?
Christ Jesus, it is He;
Lord Sabaoth is His name,
From age to age the same,
And He must win the battle.

And though this world, with devils filled,
Should threaten to undo us,
We will not fear, for God hath willed
His truth to triumph through us.
The prince of darkness grim —
We tremble not for him;
His rage we can endure,
For lo! his doom is sure:
One little word shall fell him.

That word above all earthly powers —
No thanks to them — abideth;
The Spirit and the gifts are ours
Thro' Him who with us sideth.
Let goods and kindred go,
This mortal life also;
The body they may kill;
God's truth abideth still,
His kingdom is forever.

5. **ONWARD, CHRISTIAN SOLDIERS**
Onward, Christian Soldiers!
Marching as to war,
With the cross of Jesus
Going on before;
Christ, the royal Master,
Leads against the foe;
Forward into battle,
See, His banners go!

Refrain:
Onward, Christian soldiers,
Marching as to war,
With the cross of Jesus
Going on before!

Like a mighty army
Moves the Church of God;
Brothers, we are treading
Where the saints have trod;
We are not divided;
All one body we,
One in hope and doctrine,
One in charity. **Refrain**

Crowns and thrones may perish,
Kingdoms rise and wane,
But the Church of Jesus
Constant will remain.
Gates of hell can never
'Gainst that Church prevail;
We have Christ's own promise,
And that cannot fail. **Refrain**

Onward, then, ye people,
Join our happy throng,
Blend with ours your voices
In the triumph song;
Glory, laud, and honor,
Unto Christ the King:
This thro' countless ages
Men and angels sing. **Refrain**

6. **HOLY, HOLY, HOLY, LORD GOD ALMIGHTY**
Holy, Holy, Holy, Lord God Almighty!
Early in the morning our song shall rise to
    Thee;
Holy, Holy, Holy! Merciful and Mighty!
God in Three Persons, blessed Trinity!

Holy, Holy, Holy! All the saints adore Thee,
Casting down their golden crowns around the
    glassy sea;
Cherubim and seraphim falling down before
    Thee,
Who wert, and art, and evermore shalt be.

Holy, Holy, Holy. Tho' the darkness hide
    Thee,
Tho' the eye of sinful man Thy glory may
    not see,
Only Thou art holy; there is none beside
    Thee
Perfect in pow'r, in love, in purity.

Holy, Holy, Holy, Lord God Almighty!
All Thy works shall praise Thy name in
    earth, and sky, and sea;
Holy, Holy, Holy! Merciful and Mighty!
God in Three Persons, blessed Trinity!

7. **FAIREST LORD JESUS**
Fairest Lord Jesus,
Ruler of all nature,
O Thou of God and man the Son,
Thee will I cherish,
Thee will I honor,
Thou my soul's glory, joy, and crown.

Fair are the meadows,
Fairer still the woodlands,
Robed in the blooming garb of spring;
Jesus is fairer,
Jesus is purer,
Who makes the woeful heart to sing.

Fair is the sunshine,
Fairer still the moonlight,
And all the twinkling, starry host;
Jesus shines brighter,
Jesus shines purer,
Than all the angels heaven can boast.

8. **NEARER, MY GOD TO THEE**
Nearer, my God, to Thee,
Nearer to Thee!
E'en though it be a cross
That raiseth me;
Still all my song shall be,
Nearer, my God, to Thee,
Nearer, my God, to Thee,
Nearer to Thee!

Though like the wanderer,
The sun gone down,
Darkness be over me,
My rest a stone;
Yet in my dreams I'd be
Nearer, my God, to Thee,
Nearer, my God, to Thee,
Nearer to Thee!

There let the way appear,
Steps unto heaven:
All that Thou sendest me,
In mercy given:
Angels to beckon me
Nearer, my God, to Thee,
Nearer, my God, to Thee,
Nearer to Thee!

Then with my waking thoughts
Bright with Thy praise,
Out of my stony griefs
Bethel I'll raise;
So by my woes to be
Nearer, my God, to Thee,
Nearer, my God, to Thee,
Nearer to Thee!

Or if on joyful wing,
Cleaving the sky,
Sun, moon, and stars forgot,
Upward I fly,
Still all my song shall be,
Nearer, my God, to Thee,
Nearer, my God, to Thee,
Nearer to Thee!

9. **FACE TO FACE**
Face to face with Christ my Saviour,
Face to face — what will it be —
When with rapture I behold Him,
Jesus Christ who died for me?

Refrain:
Face to face I shall behold Him,
Far beyond the starry sky;
Face to face in all His glory,
I shall see him by and by.

Only faintly now I see Him,
With the darkling veil between;
But a blessed day is coming,
When His glory shall be seen. **Refrain**

What rejoicing in His presence,
When are banished grief and pain;
When the crooked ways are straightened,
And the dark things shall be plain. **Refrain**

Face to face! O blissful moment!
Face to face — to see and know;
Face to face with my Redeemer,
Jesus Christ who loves me so. **Refrain**

10. **SOFTLY AND TENDERLY**
Softly and tenderly Jesus is calling,
Calling for you and for me;
See, on the portals He's waiting and
    watching,
Watching for you and for me.

Refrain:
Come home, (Come home,) Come home;
  (Come home,)
Ye who are weary, come home;
Earnestly, tenderly, Jesus is calling,
Calling, O sinner, come home!

Why should we tarry when Jesus is pleading,
Pleading for you and for me?
Why should we linger and heed not His
  mercies,
Mercies for you and for me? Refrain

Time is now fleeting, the moments are
  passing,
Passing from you and from me;
Shadows are gathering, death-beds are
  coming,
Coming for you and for me. Réfrain

Oh! for the wonderful love He has promised,
Promised for you and for me;
Tho' we have sinned, He has mercy and
  pardon,
Pardon for you and for me. Refrain

11. AMAZING GRACE
Amazing grace! how sweet the sound,
That saved a wretch like me!
I once was lost, but now am found,
Was blind, but now I see.

'Twas grace that taught my heart to fear,
And grace my fears relieved;
How precious did that grace appear
The hour I first believed!

Thru many dangers, toils and snares,
I have already come;
'Tis grace hath bro't me safe thus far
And grace will lead me home.

When we've been there ten thousand years,
Bright shining as the sun,
We've no less days to sing God's praise
Than when we first begun.

12. I LOVE TO TELL THE STORY
I love to tell the story
Of unseen things above,
Of Jesus and His glory,
Of Jesus and His love.
I love to tell the story,
Because I know 'tis true;
It satisfies my longings
As nothing else can do.

Refrain:
I love to tell the story,
'Twill be my theme in glory
To tell the old, old story
Of Jesus and His love.

I love to tell the story,
More wonderful it seems
Than all the golden fancies
Of all our golden dreams.
I love to tell the story,
It did so much for me;
And that is just the reason
I tell it now to thee. Refrain

I love to tell the story,
'Tis pleasant to repeat
What seems, each time I tell it,
More wonderfully sweet.
I love to tell the story,
For some have never heard
The message of salvation
From God's own holy word. Refrain

I love to tell the story,
For those who know it best
Seem hungering and thirsting
To hear it like the rest.
And when, in scenes of glory,
I sing the new, new song,
'Twill be the old, old story
That I have loved so long. Refrain

13. O THAT WILL BE GLORY
When all my labors and trials are o'er,
And I am safe on that beautiful shore,
Just to be near the dear Lord I adore,
Will thro' the ages be glory for me.

Refrain:
O that will be glory for me,
Glory for me, glory for me;
When by His grace I shall look on His face,
That will be glory, be glory for me.

When, by the gift of His infinite grace,
I am accorded in heaven a place,
Just to be there and to look on His face,
Will thro' the ages be glory for me. Refrain

Friends will be there I have loved long ago;
Joy like a river around me will flow;
Yet, just a smile from my Savior, I know,
Will thro' the ages be glory for me. Refrain

14. JESUS, LOVER OF MY SOUL
Jesus, Lover of my soul,
Let me to Thy bosom fly,
While the nearer waters roll,
While the tempest still is high:
Hide me, O my Saviour, hide,
Till the storm of life is past;
Safe into the haven guide;
O receive my soul at last!

Other refuge have I none;
Hangs my helpless soul on Thee;
Leave, ah! leave me not alone,
Still support and comfort me.
All my trust on Thee is stayed,
All my help from Thee I bring;
Cover my defenseless head
With the shadow of Thy wing.

Thou, O Christ, art all I want;
More than all in Thee I find:
Raise the fallen, cheer the faint,
Heal the sick, and lead the blind.
Just and holy is Thy name;
I am all unrighteousness;
False and full of sin I am,
Thou art full of truth and grace.

Plenteous grace with Thee is found,
Grace to cover all my sin;
Let the healing streams abound;
Make and keep me pure within.
Thou of life the Fountain art,
Freely let me take of Thee;
Spring Thou up within my heart.
Rise to all eternity.

15. BLESSED ASSURANCE
Blessed assurance, Jesus is mine!
O what a foretaste of glory divine!
Heir of salvation, purchase of God,
Born of His Spirit, washed in His blood.

Refrain:
This is my story, this is my song,
Praising my Saviour all the day long;
This is my story, this is my song,
Praising my Saviour all the day long.

Perfect submission, perfect delight,
Visions of rapture now burst on my sight!
Angels descending, bring from above
Echoes of mercy, whispers of love. Refrain

Perfect submission, all is at rest,
I in my Saviour am happy and blest;
Watching and waiting, looking above,
Filled with His goodness, lost in His love.
Refrain

16. HE LEADETH ME
He leadeth me! O blessed tho't!
O words with heav'nly comfort fraught!
Whate'er I do, where'er I be,
Still 'tis God's hand that leadeth me.

Refrain:
He leadeth me, He leadeth me,
By His own hand He leadeth me:
His faithful follower I would be,
For by His hand He leadeth me.

Sometimes 'mid scenes of deepest gloom,
Sometimes where Eden's bowers bloom,
By waters still, o'er troubled sea,
Still 'tis my God that leadeth me! Refrain

Lord, I would clasp Thy hand in mine,
Nor ever murmur nor repine,
Content, whatever lot I see,
Since 'tis my God that leadeth me! Refrain

And when my task on earth is done,
When, by Thy grace, the victry's won,
E'en death's cold wave I will not flee,
Since God thro' Jordan leadeth me. Refrain

17. FAITH OF OUR FATHERS
Faith of our fathers! living still
In spite of dungeon, fire and sword,
O how our hearts beat high with joy

Whene'er we hear that glorious word!
Faith of our fathers! holy faith!
We will be true to thee till death!

Our fathers, chained in prisons dark,
Were still in heart and conscience free:
How sweet would be their children's fate,
If they, like them, could die for thee!
Faith of our fathers! holy faith!
We will be true to thee till death!

Faith of our fathers, God's great power
Shall win all nations unto thee,
And through the truth that comes from God
Mankind shall then indeed be free.
Faith of our fathers, holy faith,
We will be true to thee till death.

Faith of our fathers! we will love
Both friend and foe in all our strife:
And preach thee, too, as love knows how,
By kindly words and virtuous life:
Faith of our fathers! holy faith!
We will be true to thee till death!

18. SWEET HOUR OF PRAYER
Sweet hour of prayer! sweet hour of prayer!
That calls me from a world of care,
And bids me at my Father's throne
Make all my wants and wishes known;
In seasons of distress and grief,
My soul has often found relief,
And oft escaped the tempter's snare
By thy return, sweet hour of prayer.

Sweet hour of prayer! sweet hour of prayer!
Thy wings shall my petition bear
To Him whose truth and faithfulness
Engage the waiting soul to bless;
And since He bids me seek His face,
Believe His Word and trust His grace,
I'll cast on Him my every care,
And wait for thee, sweet hour of prayer.

Sweet hour of prayer! sweet hour of prayer!
May I thy consolation share,
Till, from Mount Pisgah's lofty height,
I view my home, and take my flight:
This robe of flesh I'll drop, and rise
To seize the everlasting prize;
And shout, while passing through the air,
Farewell, farewell, sweet hour of prayer.

19. BLEST BE THE TIE THAT BINDS
Blest be the tie that binds
Our hearts in Christian love;
The fellowship of kindred minds
Is like to that above.

Before our Father's throne
We pour our ardent pray'rs;
Our fears, our hopes, our aims are one,
Our comforts and our cares.

We share each other's woes,
Each other's burdens bear;
And often for each other flows
The sympathizing tear.

When we are called to part
It gives us inward pain;
But we shall still be joined in heart,
And hope to meet again.

From sorrow, toil, and pain,
And sin, we shall be free;
And perfect love and friendship reign
Through all eternity.

20. ABIDE WITH ME
Abide with me: fast falls the eventide;
The darkness deepens; Lord, with me abide:
When other helpers fail, and comforts flee,
Help of the helpless, O abide with me!

Swift to its close ebbs out life's little day;
Earth's joys grow dim, its glories pass away;
Change and decay in all around I see:
O Thou who changest not, abide with me!

I need Thy presence every passing hour:
What but Thy grace can foil the tempter's
  power?
Who like Thyself my guide and stay can be?
Through cloud and sunshine, O abide with me!

Hold Thou Thy word before my closing eyes;
Shine through the gloom, and point me to
  the skies:
Heaven's morning breaks, and earth's vain
  shadows flee
In life, in death, O Lord, abide with me!